Praise for
WALKING IN WONDER

"How glorious it is to hear the voice of John O'Donohue again, the lark-tongued poet, philosopher, theologian and *anam cara,* who left his imprint on everyone he met. Anyone who spent time with him—in person or in books—came away changed. In this spirited conversation, John is fiercely alive with the electric fizz of being, fully attuned to life, ruminative, and so infused with wonder that every question becomes a lantern. As ever, he delves deeply into the plateaus of being human, and explores the thresholds that arise, frighten, but must be crossed to become the self one dreams. I so cherish this unexpected gift."

—Diane Ackerman, author of *The Zookeeper's Wife*

"As this magnificent book demonstrates, even on the printed page John O'Donohue's voice—so lyrical and eloquent, so profound and impassioned—flashes vividly to life, beautifully capturing a radiant soul filled with humor, compassion and utter selflessness. Indeed, John not only brilliantly articulated the magic and necessity of joy and gratitude, he ignited a sense of genuine awe in every life he encountered, and he will undoubtedly inspire future generations to learn how to infuse their own lives with meaning and wonder."

—Andrew Carroll, *New York Times* bestselling author and the cofounder, with the Nobel laureate Joseph Brodsky, of the American Poetry & Literacy Project

"John Quinn's self-effacing work as editor and broadcaster is rightly renowned. Here he presents, for wider audiences, his absorbing conversations with John O'Donohue's glorious, far-seeing, far-reaching spirit. Welcome to these luminous encounters!"

—Lelia Doolan, Irish activist in various fields

"In these conversations, John Donohue's timely words feed the deep spiritual hunger that creeps into our hearts as individuals and our nation as a whole. He reframes the human story of fear, aging, death, otherness and absence, reminding us that they are all bound up in the mystery of wonder. O'Donohue lives on as a prophetic and priestly presence for such a time as this."

—Rev. Dr. Katharine Henderson, president of Auburn Seminary

"In each chapter the reader experiences a rich and exhilarating new conversation. We witness a man whose intellect and life force are in full bloom, deeply rooted in spirit, humor, curiosity and compassion. John invites us to pause and reflect, challenging us to reach beyond our well-trod and comfortable assumptions."

—Richard Harrell, musician and educator at the Juilliard School, San Francisco Conservatory, and Orfeo Foundation

"Luminous! *Walking in Wonder* shines light on life's dark mysteries and offers sustenance for spiritual hunger. As you confront the inevitable thresholds of loss, absence and aging, this book will serve as a road map to help you navigate with grace, gratitude and a fearless heart. John O'Donohue's elegant words are a call to live with abundance, to look inward with courage and to look outward with compassion. They are a reminder to embrace the wild energy of your soul."

—Gina Vild, coauthor of *The Two Most Important Days: How to Find Your Purpose—and Live a Happier, Healthier Life*

"John O'Donohue's insights in this new collection offer a glimpse into the wonder and presence of knowing him. His signature themes rooted in Celtic spirituality and contemplative exploration offer breadcrumbs on the path, encouraging us to embrace the beauty and gift of each day."

—Davy Spillane, Grammy Award–winning musician and composer at North Atlantic Music, Ireland

"This volume is a testament to the timelessness of John O'Donohue's wisdom. His words are not only inspirational to those of us catalyzing substantive social change but compel us to consider how we nurture, support and thrive amidst chaos."

—Rev. Diane J. Johnson, PhD, national interfaith and social justice activist, and founder and president of Mmapeu Management Consulting

WALKING IN WONDER

WALKING IN WONDER

Eternal Wisdom for a Modern World

JOHN O'DONOHUE

IN CONVERSATION WITH JOHN QUINN

Foreword by Krista Tippett

CONVERGENT
New York

Published in the United States by Convergent Books,
an imprint of the Crown Publishing Group,
a division of Penguin Random House LLC, New York.
convergentbooks.com

CONVERGENT BOOKS is a registered trademark and its C colophon is a trademark of Penguin Random House LLC.

Originally published in hardcover and in slightly different form in Ireland by Veritas Publications, Dublin, in 2015.

Library of Congress Cataloging-in-Publication Data
Names: O'Donohue, John, 1956–2008. author. | Quinn, John, 1941– author.
Title: Walking in wonder: eternal wisdom for a modern world / John O'Donohue and John Quinn.
Description: New York: Penguin Random House, 2018.
Identifiers: LCCN 2018012916 (print) | LCCN 2018038223 (ebook) | ISBN 9780525575290 (e-book) | ISBN 9780525575283 (hardcover)
Subjects: LCSH: Spirituality. | Mysticism.
Classification: LCC B105.S64 (ebook) | LCC B105.S64 O358 2018 (print) | DDC 242—dc23
LC record available at https://lccn.loc.gov/2018012916

ISBN 978-0-525-57528-3
Ebook ISBN 978-0-525-57529-0

PRINTED IN THE UNITED STATES OF AMERICA

Jacket design by Sarah Horgan
Jacket and chapter opener illustration by Mikhail Zyablov/Shutterstock
Jacket photograph by mammuth/E+/Getty Images

10 9 8 7 6 5 4 3 2

First U.S. Edition

CONTENTS

CONTENTS

FOREWORD

By Krista Tippett

IN THE FALL OF 2007, I SPENT THREE HOURS IN conversation with John O'Donohue in my studio in St. Paul. It was an incomparably intense, pleasurable and vast experience. I would say to friends later that it was as though this man had five answers for every question—five layers of thinking for each of his geologic layers of personality: the poet in him, the philosopher, the theologian, the Irish bard and the splendid, searching, openly ragged-around-the-edges human being. He was not easy to edit for the radio hour.

After the turn of that year, just as we prepared to put his voice on the air, word came that John had died. I found his death hard to comprehend. He was one of the most alive beings I had encountered. I could not imagine his absence from the world. And now the conversation I had with him became intertwined with his passing. It was how many learned he had died. It aired in Los Angeles just as a group of John's close friends were en route to a gathering to remember him. The timing was uncanny, they said, and yet somehow perfectly in character: as though John had invited himself to his own memorial service and made sure it was lit by his passion and poetry and joy.

This book you now hold in your hands is a treasure. Since I discovered its original Ireland edition, it has rarely left my side. It is John's voice with us anew and as always and again, as I encountered him, in the sacramental acts he made of thinking and conversing. It is beautifully woven of John ruminating with his dear friend John Quinn. It is sprinkled with his blessings and his poetry and even wise reflections he made on the aging he never really got to. Page after page illustrates John's insistence that "all thinking that is imbued with wonder is graceful and gracious thinking."

This book appears to us, though, in a transfigured moment in the life of the world. John's diagnosis of our estrangement from the loved ones and strangers with whom we share our lives and our lands directly addresses our unfolding century. "The media," he writes, "is essentially like Plato's Cave—a parade of shadows that we take for the real world. It is a huge abstraction from what is real."

This was as true in his lifetime as it is in ours, but most of us were not yet ready to grapple as openly as we now must with its consequences.

Likewise, we are perhaps more ready now to take in John's wisdom that life together is an existential and spiritual calling more than it is a political one. Fear, he reminds us in a fearful season, derives its power from the fragility of the human heart. It is "negative wonder"— "the point at which wonder begins to consume itself and scrape off the essence of things."

I hear all the time how John's voice in many forms continues to walk with far-flung humans through despair and illness and healing and renewal—helping us, in his gorgeous way with words, cross those thresholds more worthily. In death, John O'Donohue has made real the mysterious, vital interplay he taught in his life, between the material and the spiritual, the visible and the invisible worlds. This book deepens the miracle of his presence that is only becoming more vivid and more necessary.

INTRODUCTION

WHEN JOHN O'DONOHUE DIED SUDDENLY IN January 2008, he left a deep void in the hearts and minds of many people. For more than a decade prior to his death, his writings, talks and broadcasts had done much to feed the "unprecedented spiritual hunger" that he had observed in modern society. His books on Celtic spirituality were bestsellers; his broadcasts and talks tapped into the needs of the sizable audiences that tuned into them.

Over a period of five years I was privileged to work with John on a variety of radio programs. We climbed Mámean mountain in Connemara for "This Place Speaks to Me." We discussed Meister Eckhart as his choice of "Millennium Minds." We explored aging and death for the series "L Plus." We spoke about wonder for "The Open Mind," and John delivered the 1997 Open Mind Guest Lecture on the theme of absence. Our loss of John is tempered by the legacy of these broadcasts and I am indebted to Veritas for making them available in print and to RTÉ for originally broadcasting them, as well as to John's family. I have interspersed between the sections some of John's "Blessings" from his book *To Bless the Space Between Us*.

Wonder, imagination and possibility were John's great concerns, and he articulated them in his own inimitable lyrical style. The rich flow of his language—cadences, rhythms, colloquial flavoring—were a large part of John's attraction to his radio audience. This poses a dilemma, however, when translating radio programs into print. Do you edit transcripts heavily—almost rewrite them—to accommodate the print medium? Or do you leave them relatively intact, faithful to the original? We have opted for the latter, in the belief that John's words still sing off the page. We hope that you, the reader, will concur.

Whatever the medium, there are great riches here— the product of a brilliant mind, a mind that never stopped striving to advance the frontiers of possibility.

John Quinn

WONDER

"So many people are frightened by the
wonder of their own presence."

In 1997, I devised a summer series for RTÉ
Radio—"Webs of Wonder." Each program
would comprise moments of wonder—
archive pieces, poetry, music—but I also
needed some philosophical pieces to act
as the threads that held the web together.
So I went to John O'Donohue. We met in
the bar of a hotel in Kinvara, Co. Galway,
and talked for an hour about many aspects
of wonder—imagination, transience, landscape. In the course of the conversation,

John came up with the lovely phrase that gave me the title for this book—"the pastures of wonder." It was a quiet evening in the bar. Nobody disturbed the recording. Just two fellows chatting in the corner of a bar. It was wonderful. Wonder-ful.

GATEWAYS TO WONDER

One of the fascinating things about humans is that, in contrast to stones and to water and to earth and to fields, they seem to be privileged and burdened with the ability to think. That's the beautiful intimacy of the human in the world. There is nothing as intimate as a human being. Every human person is inevitably involved with two worlds: the world they carry within them and the world that is out there. All thinking, all writing, all action, all creation and all destruction is about that bridge between the two worlds. All thought is about putting a face on experience. Socrates said that the unexamined life isn't worth living. Socrates started raising the questions. One of the most exciting and energetic forms of thought is the question. I always think that the question is like a lantern. It illuminates new landscapes and new areas as it moves. Therefore, the question always assumes that there are many different dimensions to a thought that you are either blind to or that are not available to you. So a question is really one of the forms in which wonder expresses itself. One of the reasons that we wonder is because we are limited, and that limitation is one of the great gateways of wonder. Martin Heidegger said that when you can conceive of a frontier you are already beyond it, because a frontier—while it may be the limitation of where you now are or what you now feel or think—is also the threshold of what you are actually going to move into. This is put very lyrically and beautifully by a great rustic poet, our own Patrick Kavanagh, who said in his amazing "Advent" poem, "Through a chink too wide there comes in no wonder." That means that in a certain sense, the narrower and more confined the chink or the crevice or the opening, the greater the possibility of wonder actually is. All thinking that is imbued with wonder is graceful and gracious thinking. Thought is at the heart of reality. All of the things that we do, the things that we see, touch, feel, are all constructions of thought. When you think about a city, everything in that city is an expression of thought. Hands and machines created the things, but thought was actually the forerunner of all that. And thought, if it's not open to wonder, can be limiting, destructive and very, very dangerous. If you look at thought as a circle, and if half the arc of the circle is the infusion of wonder, then the thought will be kind, it will be gracious, and it will also be compassionate, because wonder and compassion are sisters. Each one of us is the custodian of an inner world that we carry around with us. Now, other people can glimpse it from the way we behave, the way our language is and particularly the way that our face and our eyes are. But no one but you knows what your inner world is actually like, and no one can force you to reveal it until you actually tell them about it. That's the whole mystery of writing and language and expression—that when you do say it, what others hear and what you intend and know are often totally different kinds of things. So each one of us is privileged to be the custodian of this inner world, which is accessible only through thought, and we are also doomed, in the sense that we cannot unshackle ourselves from the world that we actually carry. Therefore, I think that all human being and human identity and human growth is about finding some kind of balance between the privilege and the doom or the inevitability of carrying this kind of world.

THE ANIMAL WORLD

I think one of the terribly destructive areas of Western thought is that we have excluded animals from the soul, the awareness and the thought world. I feel that animals are maybe more refined than us, and that part of the recognition and respect for the animal is to acknowledge that they inhabit a different universe from us. There are sheep and rabbits and cows in the village I live in, in Connemara, and none of them know anything about Jesus, about the Buddha, about Wall Street, about zero tolerance. They are just in another world altogether. Part of the wonder of the human mind is when you look towards animals with respect and reverence, you begin to feel the otherness of the world that they actually carry. It must take immense contemplative discipline to be able to hold a world stirring within you and to have no means to express it, because animals in the main are silent and they don't have access to the paradoxical symbolic nuance of language as we have. So I use the word "contemplative" about them in that sense. For me, they are a source of a great kind of wonder. Now, that doesn't mean that I romanticize them—I was born on a farm and I know farming very well and I know the other dark side of the animal world too—but there is something really to be wondered at, at the way that they move and the way that they are. Where I envy animals is that I don't think they are haunted by consciousness in the way that humans are. I think that one of the most beautiful and frightening days in the life of a human person is when their mind really wakes up. Often when you watch a new baby or a little child, you see that they're still within the pastures of wonder and innocence. Then you think of them coming out of that, and traveling the longest journey that all of us have made—the journey of innocence to experience through adolescence. But that isn't really the worst journey. The worst and most frightening moment is the day that your mind really wakes up and that you suddenly know that everything that you think, everything that you feel, everything that you know and everything that you are connected with is somehow dependent on your awareness and your consciousness. You know that if you are graced with creative and compassionate and warm awareness, you are going to have an incredible life. You are going to have sufferings as well, but you will always return to that place of warmth and fire within yourself. But you know too on that day that if your awareness goes away or if it gets into the totally chaotic, symbolic world of otherness that we call madness, that you are totally gone. I often think of people in mental institutions. They are living in a jungle of symbols for which there is no map or grammar, and they are people who are totally instantaneous and totally haunted by a negative, distraught kind of wonder. There are many dimensions of human life that journalism, the media, religion and politics never advert to, marginal places where incredible soul-presence and soul-making and soul-creativity are always secretly at work. Ezra Pound said something like that when he said that beauty always shuns the public places—where the light is too garish and where there is no shelter—but it goes to the out-of-the-way, unknown places because only there will it encounter the reverence and hospitality of gaze that is worthy of it. Or again, to paraphrase Kavanagh: "the chink is too wide."

TRANSIENCE

One of the most amazing recognitions of the human mind is that time passes. Everything that we experience somehow passes into a past invisible place: when you think of yesterday and the things that were troubling you and worrying you, and the intentions that you had and the people that you met, and you know you experienced them all, but when you look for them now, they are nowhere—they have vanished. One of the questions that has always puzzled me is, is there a place where our vanished days secretly gather? To put it another way, like the medieval mystics used to ask, where does the light go when the candle is blown out? It seems to me that our times are very concerned with experience, and that nowadays to hold a belief, to have a value must be woven through the loom of one's own experience, and that experience is the touchstone of integrity, verification and authenticity. And yet the destiny of every experience is that it will disappear. It's a great consolation of course that things do actually disappear, especially when you feel bad. There was a contest of wisdom one time in ancient Greece to find who could write down a sentence which would somehow always be true. The sentence that won the competition was "This too will pass." One of my favorite thinkers in the feminine and mystical tradition is Teresa of Avila. She cautioned that in bad, lonesome, difficult times, you should never forget that this too will actually pass. So there is a shelter and a kindness in that acknowledgment of transience. But there's also a desperate loneliness in transience, in knowing the one that you love, the beautiful time that you are having, the lovely things that are happening to you will all actually disappear.

MEMORY

So is there a place where our vanished days secretly gather? I think there is, and I believe the name of that place is memory. Memory to me is one of the great sources, one of the great treasure houses, of wonder. You look at humans walking around on streets, in houses, in churches, out in fields, and you realize that each one of these creatures is carrying within herself or himself a whole harvest of lived experience. You can actually go back within yourself to great things that have happened to you and enjoy them and allow them to shelter and bless you again. One of the negative aspects of contemporary life is that there is such disrespect for memory. Memory is now attributed to computers, but computers do not have memory—they have hijacked the notion. Memory now seems to be focused almost exclusively on past woundedness and hurt, some of it induced, some of it real. It's sad that people don't use their good memories and revisit again and again the harvest of memory that is within them, and live out of the riches of that harvest, rather than out of the poverty of their woundedness. Hegel, a philosopher I love, said, "The wounds of the spirit heal and they leave no scars." If we can somehow bring the difficult things with us into the realm and the light of our souls, it is unbelievable the healing that will achieve itself in us. I think that we are infinitely greater than our minds and we are infinitely more than our images of ourselves. One of the sad things today is that so many people are frightened by the wonder of their own presence. They are dying to tie themselves into a system, a role, or to an image, or to a predetermined identity that other people have actually settled on for them. This identity may be totally at variance with the wild energies that are rising inside in their souls. Many of us get very afraid and we eventually compromise. We settle for something that is safe, rather than engaging the danger and the wildness that is in our own hearts. We should never forget that death is waiting for us. A man in Connemara said one time to a friend of mine, *Beidh muid sínte siar, a dúirt sé, cúig mhilliúin bliain déag faoin chré—* we'll be lying down in the earth for about fifteen million years, and we have a short exposure. I feel that when you recognize that death is on its way, it is a great liberation, because it means that you can in some way feel the call to live everything that is within you. One of the greatest sins is the unlived life, not to allow yourself to become chief executive of the project you call your life, to have a reverence always for the immensity that is inside of you. Nietzsche saw with devastating clarity the collusion that society actually is. He stripped back the layers of lies, pretension and gamesmanship, and he got down to the wild flow of energy in the well of the soul. It is impossible as a humanoid to stop the well of energy and the well of light and the well of life that is inside you. You might calm it and quell it, but it will still rise up within you.

FRIENDSHIP

Friendship in particular should be a wonderful kind of togetherness where each of the friends encourages and liberates each other into the fullness of their own potential.

Friends very often become habitual with each other and they limit the potential of their friendship. If you feel with your friend that you are called to the outer frontiers, then the friendship is in growth, and it also has a bit of danger in it, and a risk; and without risk in the world of the soul, nothing really grows. It's lovely when you meet people that were maybe very set in their days and in their ways, and maybe because of illness, or because of friendship or love, or some kind of awakening, suddenly the scene changes and they acknowledge, as Antonio Machado, the Spanish poet, says, that they are now in a different world. That sense of difference and otherness is always what makes us wonder. When I see predictability and habit and similarity, I am always wondering what is hidden underneath. Or when I see really good people, or really good families, I ask myself, where is the dark stuff hidden here? What is buried under the gleaming surface? Because every image is partial, and most images have a great falsity in them. When you get below the image level to the river of otherness and difference that is in every soul, that is when your eyes fill with wonder. You realize that maybe just for a little second, you are getting a glimpse of another world that is somehow there behind what you thought you knew. The Colombian writer Gabriel García Márquez was asked by his friend and fellow writer Mendoza, in a wonderful collection of conversations, what did he think of his wife, Mercedes? Márquez, who has been with Mercedes for forty years now, said to Mendoza, "I know her so well now, that I haven't the slightest idea who she is." I think that is familiarity as an invitation to absolute wonder.

FEAR

Fear is a force that can turn that which is real, meaningful, warm, gentle and kind in your life into devastation and desert. It is a powerful force. Fear derives its power also from time and from the fragility of the human heart. Because there is both time and distance between us and everything else inside us, very often the way we are towards these things becomes fearful because we get insecure. To link in with the theme of this conversation, I feel that fear is negative wonder. It is the point at which wonder begins to consume itself and scrape off the essence of things. It begins to people realities with ghost figures. It makes the self feel vulnerable and it can take away all the loveliness from your experience and from your friendships, and even from your action and your work. The reason fear has so much power is that fear is the sister of death, and that death works through fear an awful lot. I don't believe that death comes at the end of life. I believe your death was there at your birth with you. It was the unknown presence. Every step of the road of your life that you take, your death is beside you. Death often works through the vehicle of fear, so as you begin to transfigure your own fear, you are actually transfiguring the presence of your own death. At the end of your life, when death comes, it won't be some kind of monster forcefully expelling you from the familiar into the unknown, but it can actually be a friend who hides the most truthful image of your own soul. Each day, however, you have to work at transfiguring the fear.

The best story I know about fear is a story from India. It is several thousand years old, and it is a story about a man who was condemned to spend a night in a cell with a poisonous snake. If he made the slightest little stir, the snake was on top of him and he was dead. So he stood in the corner of the cell, opposite where the snake was, and he was petrified. He barely dared to breathe for fear of alerting the snake, and he stood stiff and petrified all night long. As the first bars of light began to come into the cell at dawn, he began to make out the shape of the snake, and he was saying to himself, wasn't I lucky that I never stirred. But when the full force of light came in with the full dawn, he noticed that it wasn't a snake at all. It was an old rope. Now the story is banal, but the moral of the story is very profound: in a lot of the rooms of our minds, there are harmless old ropes thrown in corners, but when our fear begins to work on them, we convert them into monsters who hold us prisoners in the bleakest, most impoverished rooms of our hearts. Outside these rooms there are glories waiting for us, but we remain transfixed in the panic of fear's awful falsity.

LIGHT

What is the source of the light that banishes our fear? I read a lovely sentence in a Hindu book years ago which said, consciousness always shines with the light from beyond itself. One of my images of the divine is that it is light in some form, and that the divine light works very tenderly with human freedom. If you don't believe that the light is there, you will experience the darkness. But if you believe the light is there, and if you call the light towards you, and if you call it into whatever you're involved in, the light will never fail you. I often think that what the heart of the Christian mystery, the Resurrection, means is that at the heart of darkness—to use Joseph Conrad's phrase—there isn't darkness but the eternal candle. In Connemara, the *seandaoine* used to say when somebody died, *Tá a choinneal múchta*, his candle is quenched. I asked an old man one day why he would say that, and he said, I often heard as a small lad that when you're born, there's a candle lit for you in the eternal world, and the length of your life is the length of the candle! Thought, creative thought particularly, is about quarrying for or liberating light. There is light inside in everything that happens to you.

One of the really sad things is when people get involved in situations in their relationships where it becomes totally destructive, and where they fix on each other on the mutual points of gravity and poverty. It is so hard for them to believe that hidden in the heart of this poverty, there is light. Much of our impoverishment derives precisely and directly from a failure of imagination, because there is some very tenuous and very special linkage between expectation and gift. If you do expect something with reverence and compassion, it will come towards you and be given to you. The proof of that is, people who have been through hell on this earth, and it still somehow hasn't tarnished or dulled their essence. Within the awfulness that was happening to them, they were somehow given the grace to find the buried light and it minded them. As it is said in the Bible, "Not a hair on your head will be harmed." I think of that lovely phrase "Do not be afraid"; it is repeated 366 times in the Bible. That is once for every day and, as somebody said, once for no reason at all!

SHELTER

There is a special shelter around every person. One of the things that all children should be taught when they are growing up is that there is a shelter around them, but that they won't feel the shelter if they don't expect it and if they don't know that it is there. That shelter is the shelter of your soul, it is the shelter of your God and it is the shelter of your angel. I know that angels are back in fashion now, and a lot of the thinking about angels is very soft thinking. I feel that there is given to each of us an angel's spirit to shelter and protect us and mind us. If you don't think that spirit is beside you, then you may never feel its presence, but if you do begin to tune into it and become aware of it, you will be astounded at the gentleness, the encouragement and the inspiration that your angel will bring you. There is some beautiful work done by an American psychologist called David Miller on the whole idea of angels and inspiration. One of the great places of wonder is inspiration. The lovely thing about the concept of wonder is that it completely escapes the grid of control and predictability. It seems to witness to another sense of sourcing which cannot be programmed, which can be expected and which is always received with surprise. One of the lovely things about Anglo-Saxon linguistic philosophy is that it has made us aware of the fact that we shouldn't approach the essence of a thing by trying to get a hard definition of it. We should try more to gather the family of concepts or ideas which belong to a reality. If you look at the concept of wonder, you have presences like surprise, expectation, celebration, inspiration, unpredictability, participation, mystery. There is a wonderful German philosopher called Hans-Georg Gadamer who said in his book *Truth and Method* that a horizon is something towards which we move but it is also something that moves along with us. One nice metaphor of human growth would be that you could be always moving to a new horizon, not abandoning the former ones, but in the graciousness of memory's loyalty actually bringing them along with you so that you are coming to new places all the time. One of the lovely things about wonder is that it is also the sister of novelty and newness and freshness.

IMAGINATION

Imagination is one of the closest presences in the whole family of wonder. In a way, imagination is a quality of all these different presences, and imagination is the threshold at which they begin to emerge. Imagination never pretends to know it all. It never demands or claims an absolute standpoint, but it always relishes and celebrates the fact it is on the threshold where it cannot see everything. The kind of knowing that is in imagination is knowing through exploration. It is not predetermined concepts or ideas. I think that every person, particularly the child, has incredible imagination. When you think of the way that each of us came into the world, we were actually for the first several years of our lives absolute practitioners—every little girl and little boy was a priestess and priest of the imagination. They completely participated in the world through the power of imagination. Imagination is also very, very compassionate. It will never take one side of a polarity or a contradiction, but it will try to weave both together and to embrace them. When you look at the fact that a human always inhabits a threshold, then you see the power of imagination. Each person is always on the threshold between their inner world and their outer world, between light and darkness, between known and unknown, between question and quest, between fact and possibility. This threshold runs through every experience that we have, and our only real guide to this world is the imagination. One of the lovely things a person can do for another person is to awaken the power and sacrament of their imagination, because when you awaken someone's imagination, you are giving them a new kingdom, a new world. William Blake said that Christ is the imagination, which I think is one of the most beautiful theological statements I have ever heard. If you look at the place of Christ, the Son of God, and the whole story of the creation, he was the first "other" that ever was, and I believe, therefore, the prism of all difference that is. Imagination in the Blakeian sense is about the awakening to and the recognition of the sacredness of all the difference that is. Where the imagination is alive, wonder is completely alive. Where the imagination is alive, possibility is awake because imagination is the great friend of possibility.

Possibilities are always more interesting than facts. We shouldn't frown on facts, but our world is congested with them. Facts are retarded possibilities, they are possibilities that have already been actualized. But for every fact that becomes a fact, there are seven, eight, maybe five hundred possibilities hanging around in the background that didn't make it into the place where they could be elected and realized as the actual fact. It is very interesting to look at what you consider real and to think that it is always peopled by a background presence of unrealized possibilities. That is one of the fascinating things in going through the world—you wonder at destiny, at the way that your life actually flows and moves and grows. I have a great suspicion of an awful lot of what is paraded as moral decision and moral rectitude and moral recognition. I think there is a beautiful morality of possibility to be written, because placing all the emphasis on moral choice is very limiting. Choice is always about loss: you choose one thing over the other several things. And maybe the soul doesn't want to do that. It is a very interesting question: whether in the course of your life, you had to choose one direction, if in actual fact, unknown to you in the invisible area of your life, in the unknown area of your life, your other unchosen lives might not actually travel with you as well. Maybe one of the great surprises we will get in the wonder moment of after-death is that when we wake up and straighten up in that new kingdom, we will find that all our unchosen and unlived lives are there to welcome us as well.

LANDSCAPE

Humans have tamed landscape. They have floors, which make the ground level. There are roads and streets which make it easy to walk on. In a way, when humans are in the land, they are always on their way to somewhere else, whereas the ultimate faithfulness in life is the faithfulness of landscape. Landscape is always there. It has a Zen-like stillness to it, and when you come back after ten years or forty years, you'll always find it in the same place. That is captured in the old Irish *seanfhocal*, which says, *Castar na daoine ar a chéile, ach ní chastar na sléibhte ar a chéile*— people meet, but the mountains never actually meet.

I love mountains. I feel that mountains are huge contemplatives. They are there and they are in the presence up to their necks and they are still in it and with it and within it. One of the lovely ways to pray is to take your body out into the landscape and to be still in it. Your body is made out of clay, so your body is actually a miniature landscape that has got up from under the earth and is now walking on the normal landscape. If you go out for several hours into a place that is wild, your mind begins to slow down, down, down. What is happening is that the clay of your body is retrieving its own sense of sisterhood with the great clay of the landscape. Water in a landscape is a fascinating thing as well. I often think that water is the tears of the earth's joy and sadness. Every kind of water in a landscape has a different kind of tonality and a different kind of presence to it. You think of the stillness of a well, of the energy of a stream, of the totality of the ocean or the singularity and memory of a river. I also think that trees are incredible presences. There is incredible symmetry in a tree, between its inner life and its outer life, between its rooted memory and its external active presence. A tree grows up and grows down at once and produces enough branches to incarnate its wild divinity. It doesn't limit itself—it reaches for the sky and it reaches for the source, all in one seamless kind of movement. So I think landscape is an incredible, mystical teacher, and when you begin to tune into its sacred presence, something shifts inside you. One of the lovely developments in consciousness as we come towards the end of the millennium is this dawning recognition that we are guests of the universe, and that landscape was the firstborn of creation and was here hundreds of millions of years before us. It knows what is actually going on. To put it in a theological way, I feel that landscape is always at prayer, and its prayer is seamless. It is always enfolded in the presence. It is a high work of imagination, because there is no repetition in a landscape. Every stone, every tree, every field is a different place. When your eye begins to become attentive to this panorama of differentiation, then you realize what a privilege it is to actually be here.

For a New Beginning

In out-of-the-way places of the heart,
Where your thoughts never think to wander,
This beginning has been quietly forming,
Waiting until you were ready to emerge.

For a long time it has watched your desire,
Feeling the emptiness growing inside you,
Noticing how you willed yourself on,
Still unable to leave what you had outgrown.

It watched you play with the seduction of safety
And the gray promises that sameness whispered,
Heard the waves of turmoil rise and relent,
Wondered would you always live like this.

Then the delight, when your courage kindled,
And out you stepped onto new ground,
Your eyes young again with energy and dream,
A path of plenitude opening before you.

Though your destination is not yet clear
You can trust the promise of this opening;
Unfurl yourself into the grace of beginning
That is at one with your life's desire.

Awaken your spirit to adventure;
Hold nothing back, learn to find ease in risk;
Soon you will be home in a new rhythm
For your soul senses the world that awaits you.

From *To Bless the Space Between Us*

MEISTER ECKHART

"There is a lonely edge to our lives
which can only be filled by God."

As the second millennium drew to a
close, I conceived the idea of a series
entitled "Millennium Minds." Who were
the "great minds" of the millennium and
why? I put that question to a range of contributors and they chose a wide selection of
minds—poets, economists, composers, pol-
iticians, saints. John O'Donohue chose an
obscure medieval mystic . . .

MEISTER ECKHART IS FOR ME ONE OF THE MOST fascinating minds of the Western tradition—a mind that had its flowering in the early part of the millennium. He was a priest, a mystic—and officially a heretic!

Several people had recommended Eckhart to me over the years, and while looking around for mystical reading I stumbled on his sermons in a London bookshop. When I finished my doctorate on Hegel, my professor in Tübingen University suggested a post-doctorate dissertation on Eckhart. In the little town I was living in at the time, there was an antiquarian bookshop run by a cranky little man, a very conservative type. I happened to ask him one morning if he had anything on Eckhart. He disappeared upstairs and came back with seventeen dust-covered volumes which he had had for years. It seemed providential, so I set to work on Meister Eckhart.

A PEN PICTURE

Eckhart was born around 1260 in the village of Hochheim, near Erfurt in Germany. He became a novice at the Dominican house in Erfurt around 1277. In the 1270s he studied arts in Paris. He also studied in Cologne under Albert the Great, who had taught Thomas Aquinas. From 1293 to 1294 he lectured in Paris on the *Sentences* of Peter Lombard. In 1294 he became prior of the Dominican house in Erfurt and also vicar of the Dominican house in Thuringia. In 1302 he was called to the chair of theology in Paris, which was recognition in his time and among his peers that he was indeed a brilliant mind. From 1303 to 1311 he was the provincial of the Dominican order in Germany, and he set about reforming that province. He was back in Paris in 1311 as professor of theology. At that time too he was very active in spiritual direction around Germany. From 1322 to 1326 the first censure of his teachings took place and he made his first defense in Cologne. In 1327 he appealed to the pope, alleging delays in his trial. He went into the pulpit in Avignon (where the papacy resided) to defend himself. At that time another man, who would have no sympathy with Eckhart's teaching, William of Occam, was also defending himself. Eckhart died in 1328 and after his death the papal document *In Agro Dominico*, condemning him as a heretic, was published. What is remarkable about Eckhart is the balance in his life between the most intricate, profound intellectual work—which is particularly evident in his Latin sermons—and his very fluent and caring and involved pastoral approach. He traveled and preached widely, when travel was particularly difficult. He came after the great flowering of Greek philosophy, particularly neo-Platonist philosophy. Thomas Aquinas preceded him, so he was heir to a fascinatingly complex philosophical system.

THE IDEA OF GOD

There was a fair amount of turbulence in his time—the popes had moved to Avignon, for example. If you look at the history of thought and art, it is usually out of restless, turbulent times that great novelty and light emerge. Every great thinker is haunted by one major idea, and the delight and danger of Eckhart's mind was that his major obsession was the idea of God. That is what fired his thinking, and it ultimately brought him into conflict with the authorities at the time. To put it succinctly, Eckhart's idea of God was that there is nothing closer to us than God.

That is what made the Church suspicious of him—that he brought God too much down to earth—but in fact if you go carefully through his thought, you can see the other polarities too, that is, the incredible distance of God.

Eckhart is fascinating for us now too in that we live at a time when, I would argue, there is an unprecedented spiritual hunger. So there is an ongoing retrieval of ancient sources which have great nourishment and light in them and Eckhart is one of those sources. He believed that the identity of the human person was very intimately connected with our ability to think, so thought wasn't just a lens through which we see things, but it was our very existence and presence. He considered that God was really present in our thinking, so that when you thought of God you were not thinking about God or a distant object but you were awakening in some way the divine presence within you. When you immerse yourself in Eckhart's work and you allow your consciousness to be schooled in the cloister of his thinking, what begins to happen is that his thought, rather than being a target of your own understanding, begins to take the form of an icon which looks back at you. So the more you gaze at Eckhart's thinking, the more you feel that it actually begins to read to you. Eckhart tries to think within the divine mind, so his thought is a participation in God's presence.

A WILD GOD

The God that Eckhart believed in is an incredibly "wild" kind of God! For instance, he believed that everything had its origin in the mind of God—an old neo-Platonist idea. In every culture there are basic questions—the *what* question (what is a thing made of?), the *how* question (the process of making a thing), the *when* question (when does a thing happen?) and the luminous *who* question (who is the identity of a person?)—but one of the most fascinating questions of all concerns origins: where did things come from? The German word for this is beautiful—*woher?* Where does a thing come out of? The German word for origin is *Ursprung*—from *ur,* meaning "primal," and *springen,* "to leap," giving the idea of a primal well out of which everything sprang. For Eckhart, that place is God. When you look around and see people, landscapes, oceans, stars, birds, stones, flowers—none of them are here by accident, but each of them was born within the mind of God. In one of his beautiful Latin sermons, Eckhart says that "in the first glance of God, everything that is in the world was born." It is a very artistic notion of the divine imagination. An awful lot of theology and spirituality goes badly to ground in an excessive concentration on the will of God—poor humans trying to beat their lovely complex minds into the direction of that will—whereas Meister Eckhart tries to awaken you to the divine imagination and to help you realize that that is where you have come from, that is what holds you together in the world, that is where your ultimate destination is.

"Wild" is something you cannot tame—and I suppose one of the things institutional religion does is to have a few "official tamers" on hand in case the divine thing wakens up in too wild a way. But the beauty of mysticism is that the mystic is someone who falls in love with God and who has a sense of the pulsing presence of God which no thought, feeling or category can ever come near. The mystic keeps the God question clean of all our unworthy and inferior answers. Eckhart is "wilder" in his thinking about God than even the best atheists. What you find in him about the wilderness and absence of God is so much more profound than the kind of vacancy you find in atheistic ideas. He says that God is that wilderness in which everyone is alone. God is only our word for it, and the nearer you get to the presence the more God ceases to be God and is allowed to become completely himself. So the spiritual life is about the liberation of God from our images of him.

THE DIVINE PRESENCE

So many people get totally hooked on a certain image of God and that is where they stay. It may be a negative image of a judge who is watching you, a parental superfigure that keeps your life crippled. For Eckhart, God isn't like that at all. He is the ultimate welcome and hospitality to everything that is alive within you, so if you really live your life to the full, you are activating the presence of God within you. Eckhart also has this fascinating idea of the nothingness of everything. He talks of the *umbra nihili*, the shadow of nothingness under which all of creation stands so that there is a lonely edge to our lives which can only be filled by God. He develops the notion of the sisterhood of God and emptiness. In his wonderful teachings on detachment, he continually says that in order to come into the presence of God, you must free yourself from the grip of all external things—let things go and become completely detached. No prayer is more powerful than the prayer of the free mind, so we must unclutter our lives of all the false things which pretend to satisfy our spiritual hunger but can never actually do so. Eckhart would see our human destiny as that of awakening the presence of God within us, but also freeing ourselves of everything that is not God. He sees the soul as the place in which God is alive within us. This is very relevant for our time, as in much of contemporary American thought the soul is making something of a comeback. At school we were taught that the soul is somewhere in the body, and when the body died, the soul departed. Eckhart comes at it the other way and sees the body as being in the soul, so the soul presence both suffuses you and is all around you as well. There is a place in the soul—what Eckhart calls "the uncreated place within you"—that no darkness, shadow, suffering or separation can ever touch. If, therefore, you want to bring God alive within you, it is to that place that you must begin to journey.

Eckhart speaks beautifully of the birth of God in the soul. The incarnation of God in Jesus will make no difference to anyone if each person does not allow that birthing to happen within themselves. In an age which is very conscious of gender, it is so lovely to note that birthing is not a feminine prerogative. Both men and women can give birth to the divine within themselves. And you don't need to go anywhere to awaken to the divine presence. So many people reach outside themselves for God—to institutions, pilgrimages, statues. Eckhart claims that all this externality is governed by the world of image. The image place is the famine field, whereas if you want real nourishment you must withdraw and come into the temple of your own soul. It is there that you will awaken what is eternal within you. Eckhart talks of "coming home to your soul, to the house that you never left . . ." I often think that the spiritual journey is about the conversion of a tiny splinter of our minds. Most of our mind knows that we are eternal, but there is one small splinter which is haunted by distance and exile. If we can bring that splinter home, we can be one in God again. And once we taste the God presence, nothing else will ever satisfy.

RHYTHM

Coming back home to the place in the soul where you are completely in rhythm with yourself, with everyone else and with God, is a very difficult journey. If you get hooked on the journey and its various stages, you will probably never get home. The journey will become the goal. Eckhart very radically states that there is no such thing as a spiritual journey. It is more a question of rhythm, rather than traversing a long landscape towards the divine. When you are in rhythm with yourself, you are untouchable. You are balanced and poised. Eckhart recommends a recovery of our ancient belonging and our ancient rhythm. In most people's lives, the moment of "awakening" (as Eckhart calls it) is one of the most powerful moments that bring them back home again, out of the winter of exile where their minds would have been foraging for nourishment in the famine-fields of image. Eckhart's mysticism is a very intellectual mysticism. It believes in the power of thought as a great light and as a power that can open the doorway to your own heart. If I may recommend a book to those interested in Eckhart, it is *The Way of Paradox* by Cyprian

Smith, a Benedictine from Ampleforth College. He shows wonderfully how Eckhart's thinking can answer so many of our modern hungers.

ECKHART FOR TODAY

I love the imagination and I love thought. It is thought that makes the world intimate and takes the anonymity out of it. In the engagement with Meister Eckhart, one's thought becomes so refined and much of the dross is cleaned off. He has a lovely saying: "Thoughts are our inner senses." Just as when an external sense like sight is impaired and we cannot see properly, so if our thoughts are weak or negative or impoverished we will never see anything in ourselves. It follows that one of our great duties as humans is to develop our own thoughts, thoughts that are adequate to us and worthy of the possibilities that sleep in our souls. One of the greatest tragedies of our times is that everyone is ripping off secondhand thinking from other people, thinking that is dead and does not fit them at all. We can liberate ourselves by trusting our own instinct and finding the thought-lenses which show us our world in the way we need to see it, that can calm us and bring us home and also challenge us where we are limited or deficient or where we don't actually want to see.

Eckhart's distrust of the world of image is truly relevant

and profound. The Internet, for example, is a great facility, but as a friend said to me recently, "The fact that we have this amazing technological capability doesn't mean that good work will actually be done." I see the Internet as somewhat like Plato's allegory of the cave. All it is, ultimately, is images. It is questionable whether such abstract images ever bring the complexity and depth of people to real encounter and intimacy. Likewise, the world of public relations is like the ancient art of sophistry. Socrates fought against this notion of making the weak argument look strong—that is what public relations is about. We have created an image world and it requires someone like Eckhart, with his fire and his clarity, to break through that false wall.

Our age is also very functional. There are goals and purposes and programs for everything. The lovely thing about Eckhart is his absolute suspicion of the program. People got hooked on a program which became an end in itself. Our world today is haunted and obsessed by functional thinking which sees everything in terms of a process. Eckhart keeps God and the mystical way totally free of that thinking. He says that God is God and without a why: *non habet quare; Ipsum est quare omnium et omnibus*—He is the why of everything and to everything. A later follower of Eckhart, Angelus Silesius, wrote a beautiful short mystical poem called *"Ohne Warum"* (Without Why):

The rose is without why
She blooms because she blooms
She does not care for herself
Asks not if she is seen

One of the beautiful things in Eckhart is the idea of letting things be. So many people wonder what they should do, how they should work. For Eckhart, none of this matters. The most important thing to focus on is how you should be. That is really mindfulness of presence. All intimacy, love, belonging, creativity is not when the grubby little hands of our functional minds get into the mystery, but when we stand back and let the mystery be, become enveloped in it so that it extends us and deepens us.

Finally, Eckhart has the lovely idea of *Gelassenheit*. *Gelassen* is the German for "calmness." Even when things go against you and the rhythm in your life takes you to awkward and lonely places, you can still maintain a stillness which is in your soul and will connect you and give you an inviolable belonging and togetherness. You won't get that from a program but you can awaken it in your own heart.

For Presence

Awaken to the mystery of being here
and enter the quiet immensity of your own presence.

Have joy and peace in the temple of your senses.

Receive encouragement when new frontiers beckon.

Respond to the call of your gift and the courage to
    follow its path.

Let the flame of anger free you of all falsity.

May warmth of heart keep your presence aflame.

May anxiety never linger about you.

May your outer dignity mirror an inner dignity of
    soul.

Take time to celebrate the quiet miracles that seek
    no attention.

Be consoled in the secret symmetry of your soul.

May you experience each day as a sacred gift woven
    around the heart of wonder.

From *To Bless the Space Between Us*

LANDSCAPE

"Landscape has a soul and a presence, and landscape—living in the mode of silence—is always wrapped in seamless prayer."

For the radio series "This Place Speaks to Me," I invited contributors to choose a particular location that appealed to them and "enthuse" about that appeal in a location recording. They chose a range of sites—a town, a bog, a jail, a monastic ruin. John O'Donohue chose the "holy mountain" of Mámêan in Connemara. Mámêan has association with St. Patrick and has long been a place of pilgrimage. So it was that John and I began our pilgrimage on a misty morning in August 2000.

MÁMÉAN

On this beautiful foggy morning—the ideal landscape to see these mountains in—we are at the foot of Máméan in the middle of the Connemara mountains. There is a deep layer of cloud halfway down the mountain. The light is very mute. In certain places the morning sun is coming through the clouds, making the fog very white, and there is a stream flowing to our right, coming down the mountain. There is a great stillness. The sheep are all in their first stage of morning activity, grazing away, in their lovely Zen kind of nonchalance. We are about to ascend . . .

I wasn't born here in Connemara but I have lived here

a long time and I really find the landscape an incredible presence, a companion in my life. People often think of the Connemara landscape as very lonesome. I live in a little cottage down here, and in some strange way you are never lonesome here, because if you look out the window, there is the constant drama of the landscape unfolding before you in the different light that is always at play here. I have never known a landscape that is as dependent on light as the Connemara landscape. When the light is here the whole place is luminous and really alive with such subtlety of color. When the light goes, the landscape is so eerie and in the grip of gravity. I've always been very moved by this, and several years ago I tried to express it in a poem called "Connemara in Our Mind."

Connemara in Our Mind

It gave us
the hungry landscapes
resting upon
the unalleviated
bog-dream,

put us out
there, where
tenderness never settled,

except for the odd nest
of grouse mutterings
in the grieving rushes,

washed our eyes
in the glories of light.

In an instant
the whole place flares
in a glaze of pools,
as if a kind sun

let a red net
sink through the bog,
reach down to a forgotten
infancy of granite,
and dredge up
a haul of colors
that play and sparkle
through the smother of bog,
pinks, yellows,
amber and orange.

Your saffron scarf,
filled with wind,
rises over your head
like a halo,

then swings to catch
the back of your neck
like a sickle.

The next instant
the dark returns
this sweep of rotting land,
shrunken and vacant.

Listen,
you can almost hear
the hunger falling
back into itself.

This is no place
to be.

With the sun
withdrawn,
the bog wants to sink,
break
the anchor of rock
that holds it up.

We are left.

There is no one
who knows us.

In our monotone
we beg the bound stone
for our first echo.

From *Echoes of Memory*

In a certain way, this landscape belongs to no one, but primarily to itself. Landscape is the firstborn of creation. It was here for hundreds of millions of years before ever a plant or an animal arrived here. It was also here, obviously, before the human face ever emerged on earth. It must have seemed very strange to the ancient eye of landscape when we arrived here. Landscape has a huge, pre-human memory. It precedes everything that we know. I often think that you could talk almost of a "clay-ography": the whole biography of the earth. Everything depends of course on whether you think landscape is dead matter or whether you think it is a living presence.

I think there is life in these rocks and in these great mountains around about us, and because there is life, there is memory. The more you live among mountains like this, the more aware you become of the cadences of the place and the subtlety of the place, its presence and personality. When you look out from here this morning, you see at the front of Mámean the beginning of the Twelve Bens. The fog is halfway down the mountain, and there is another half of the mountain concealed inside that fog that the eye cannot see. With the mind you cannot penetrate that blanket of cover but with the imagination you can sense the presence that is actually there that you cannot see with the eye. And all the time, with the light and the cloud and the rain and the mist, a whole kind of narrative of presence is unfolding, hiding itself, emerging. Not alone that, one of the frightening things about Connemara for a lot of people is how lunar and how bare it actually seems. One must not forget of course that it is mainly bog, and bog is the afterlife of a forest, of all the trees that were here. So even though we are looking down now on major emptiness and bare granite mountains, there was a time when this place was completely clustered and covered with forests and trees. There is a poem that I wrote a while ago trying to reimagine that, called "The Angel of the Bog":

The Angel of the Bog

The angel of the bog mourns in the wind
That loiters all over these black meadows.

Remembers how it chose branches to strum
From the orchestra of trees that stood here;
How at twilight a chorus of birds came
To silence in nests of darkening air.

Raindrops filter through leaves, silver the air,
Wash off the film of dust to release nets
Of fragrance on which the wind can sweeten
Before expiring among the debris
That brightens each year with fallen color
Before the weight of winter seals the ground.

The dark eyes of the angel of the bog
Never open now when dawn comes to dress
The famished grass with splendid veils of red,
Amber, white, as if its soul were urgent
And young with possibility and dreams
That a vanished life might become visible.

From *Conamara Blues*

MEMORY

If the human eye had been able to look out over this land-scape maybe ten thousand years ago or more, all it would have seen would have been gray, dead black ice everywhere and everything covered completely. It must have been an incredibly frightening and suffocating experience for the land that all its color was overtaken gradually with the surge of the gray breath of the cold, and then the snow, and then the ice freezing down on top of it. To be suffo-cated under hundreds of feet of this pack ice and to have lived that way for thousands of years must have been an incredible experience for the landscape. You can imagine when the first trickles of water began to loosen and the glaciers began to move, and the landscape became freed of this whole darkness on top of it, the first time that the sun touched it, and seeds maybe hidden for thousands of years began to awaken in the earth—that must have been an incredible emergence for the landscape. So the landscape has the memory of the time of ice that the human knows nothing about; except, I believe that we are made out of clay, that in some sense that memory is within our clay as well. Maybe that is the reason that fear can get to us so quickly, that maybe what fear does is awaken this relic cold in the bone again.

We hear here behind us the tattered screeching of a

crow and we see the birds soaring in and sweeping out of the place. It is lovely to watch animals and see how at home they are in a landscape. Sheep are, I think, the undercover mystics of the Connemara landscape: I often think they are totally in a Zen mode of stillness! You would often see them, when driving the roads here, lying out in the middle of the road paying no attention to you as you slow down and pass on. They are chewing and ruminating on something totally different altogether. And there are huge populations of birds here that know these places better than the human foot or the human eye can ever know. They fit together, the landscape and the animals. The animals of course are our older brothers and sisters—they were here before we were. I often think that one of the next breakthroughs in the evolution of human consciousness will be the recognition of the subtle complexity and the hidden inner world that animals carry around with them. The innocence and silence of the animal world has a huge subtlety to it that is anything but dumb, but rather notices everything and is present in everything. Animals carry a huge ministry of witness to the silence of time and to the depth of nature. They are like the landscape in a sense: they live too in the mode of silence. It must be strange for a mountain to look at humans and the way they go around, their limbs and their eyes blurred by their desire and movement. And their inability to stay still in the one place. Pascal said that most of our troubles occur from our inability to sit still in a room, and stone manages that. Look at the stones here. They have been here for tens of thousands of years, but they don't move, they just stay still all the time. When you look out at the Twelve Bens, there is little enough distance between them, but they have never once, in hundreds of thousands of years, managed to move or to relate to one another. I often feel that there is a world, maybe an infinite world of dream, hidden at the heart of a mountain, and that maybe part of the duty of the artist is in a certain sense to excavate the secret dream world of the mountain in an imaginary way. If you do agree that landscape is alive and that it is a presence, maybe then it is in the shape of landscape, the form of mountains, that you actually get an expression of the state of the place. If you go from that perspective, then the mountains of Connemara have risen very high, almost as noble guardians of the memory of the place and as lookouts in some sense for the infinite and the eternal.

INTRUSION

This is of course a place of pilgrimage. Professor Mícheál McGréil of Maynooth has done great work here in getting a little church built, and there is a beautiful statue here by Cliodhna Cussen of St. Patrick, *Aoire Mháiméan,* with the sheep just round his legs in the stone, beautifully carved by her. On Good Friday, Mícheál McGréil leads *Stáisiúin na Croise* here and Joe John Mac an Iomaire sings that sean-nós song *Caoineadh na dTrí Mhuire,* which would break your heart with the pathos of it. I often think that our liturgies have become very bony and very spindly and have none of the sensuous textures of landscape in them. Maybe that would be one way of reviving liturgy, bringing it out into the landscape and allowing the elemental force of the landscape to clothe the liturgy again with sensuous texture and enable us to come in.

As humans, do we intrude too much on the landscape? One of the most wonderful photographers in Ireland, a person who specializes in Connemara, is Fergus Bourke. He has taken some amazing black-and-white pictures of this place. I remember one day we had exactly that conversation: what gives the person the right to intrude on this place? I suppose the only thing you can say is that the quality of your presence here in this way, in order not to be voyeuristic or consumerist, has to slow down to the level of attention where you begin to come into the rhythm of the landscape. I think Fergus Bourke's work is a witness to that, to incredible moments where he almost catches the landscape out in conversation with itself.

SILENCE

One of the things that humans have done, and especially in Western consciousness, is that we have hijacked all the primary mystical qualities for the human mind, and we have made this claim that only the human self has soul, that everything else is "de-souled" or "unsouled" as a result of that. I think that is an awful travesty, because landscape has a soul and a presence, and landscape—living in the mode of silence—is always wrapped in seamless prayer. In my book *Eternal Echoes,* I tried to explore that notion of the prayer of landscape. Meister Eckhart said that nothing in the universe resembles God so much as silence, so if you think about silence in that sense, then to come into silence is to come into the presence of the Divine. In a way, you allow yourself to be enfolded by that stillness. In a real sense, the deepest thing in a human heart is not the verbiage but is actually that still silence— not the silence of Buddhism, which often seems to me maybe something anonymous—but is the silence of intimacy where no word is needed and where a word would actually be a fracture.

To the post-modern mind, silence is terror. One of the healing ministries that a landscape performs is as a custodian of a great unclaimed silence that urbanized post-modernity has not raided yet. One of my fears would be, because of the way technology is invading space now, with the invention of virtual space and cyberspace, that we now have the commercialization of space. It is a nightmare scenario that in ten or twenty years' time, leaving Oughterard and driving that bare stretch of road here to Máméan, which is empty and vacant and has this lovely void quality, that you could be liable to drive it and have at every juncture these beamed images of things to sell or things to do! The invasion of space could actually get to that level.

DARKNESS

On the eve of the New Millennium, I wanted to try and do something special. It seemed to me to be a night that you could be alone with landscape. I went off over Black Head and spent the night on the mountain, and it was really fascinating. When you go out in a place like that on your own where humans never live, but have passed through during the day and have rarely been there in the night, you feel that you have come in to a network of sounds that you don't normally hear. At the beginning the sounds are frightening because you don't know what they are, but then you settle down with them and you feel yourself being taken into the landscape. It was lovely to watch the dawn coming out to the landscape. The moon was behind the mountain that night, and then the dawn came in on the limestone that morning. It was almost as if the sea had vacated the place; the lime was rendered so white by the new sun of the first day of the new millennium.

Here in Connemara there is a deeper kind of darkness than in the limestone of Clare, which is a very white, feminine kind of stone, sisterly, friendly in the light. Here there is kind of a light resistance and it gets very, very dark, but when it gets dark on a very cold night the sky is magnificent in terms of stars. Because you have no light pollution, you get this clarity of all these little white apertures in this big wall of darkness twinkling down at you. It is really amazing. You become aware that you are living in a universe. During the day with all the clouds, you move on because you are busy, but at night, when you get a chance to linger and really look, you become aware of the infinite distances that are out there, and the light that is reaching you now is coming to you from stars that have gone out of existence for thousands of years. It is an amazing tenderness of distance that somehow reaches you.

One of the most fascinating aspects of a landscape like this is its interior darkness. We live on the surface of the planet and there is an infinity of darkness that we rarely see. We see it when we open a grave. We create an opening where there is a huge eternal night that is never fractured by light, but lives all the time underneath us. One of the first times I encountered that as a child was when we cut turf on the bog. The first barr or layer of turf was very brown and soggy, but as you cut further down you came to the best turf, the clear black stuff. You were going back through hundreds and thousands of years finding seeds of old plants, bits of bog deal and bog oak. In a sense you were going into the memory of landscape that was totally pre-human. No writer has explored that better than Seamus Heaney in his amazing collection *North,* where he goes into the secret archive of the bog. It is done with such tight formal beauty, and there is such a sense of edge and danger to it.

WILDNESS

As humans, we need a forceful dialectic of physical, sensuous, elemental interaction with landscape. If you look at the wildlife about us—rabbits, birds, foxes—there is a seamless kind of wildness in them. There is a sense of fluency with the place they are in and the way they move in it. One of the reasons that the post-modern mind is so packed and tight is that we have lost touch with our wildness. One of the most natural ways of coming home to your wildness is to go out into a wild place. Visually, this is often evident in people's faces. Years ago, when people worked more on the land, they had a winnowed look on their faces. Now there is a great homogenization of our appearance. Similarly in the way people walked. Land people walked in a land kind of way. The spread of the land was on them, as we would say. Now more and more people walk in a corridor fashion, unlike the peasants who walked the land in their own way. I love the word "peasant." Those who use it in a derogatory manner are just uninformed, naive and vulgar. It is very difficult for people of the land to find a vocabulary for the dignity of their work and presence and belonging in the land. So much of modern opinion is fashioned in the urban world and by urban forces. How much of the television we watch refers to the land in a way that would make the people who live on the land feel they are in a noble setting? Very little, I suspect, and yet if we go back in folk consciousness there was a time when that was the most beautiful way to dwell on the earth.

WATER

Having climbed up Mámeán we have a bird's-eye view and we realize how much water there is in this landscape. There is a huge conversation in Connemara between granite and water. All around us are beautiful lakes, with mountain streams pouring into them. I love mornings after heavy rain when you hear the music of the water finding its way down the mountains. Chiffon-like streams ornament and bedeck the mountain as they weave their way. I wrote about this in a poem about Gleninagh, which is only down the road from here.

Gleninagh

The dark inside us is sistered outside
in night which dislikes the light of the face
and the colors the eye longs to embrace.

Night adores the mountain, wrapped to itself,
a giant heart beating beneath rock and grass
and a mind stilled inside one, sure thought.

Something has broken inside this Spring night,
unconsolably its rain teems unseen
onto Gleninagh Mountain's listening depth.

Next morning the light is cleansed to behold
the glad milk of thirty streams pulse and spurt
out of unknown pores in the mountain's hold.

From *Echoes of Memory*

Now it has started to mist and rain. The rain is never far away here! I welcome it because one of my fears is the way the government relentlessly nurtures the tourist industry. Ireland is a small country and if the tourist numbers aren't modified it could be overrun. Voyeuristic commercial tourism can do a lot of damage. The English scientist Rupert Sheldrake was asked what single change he would recommend for the new millennium that could make a difference to the world. His reply was that every tourist should become a pilgrim.

There is something eternal about the landscape. It wants to address us but we are not subtle enough to pick it up. The radar of our senses, while beautiful, is incredibly limited. This is illustrated for me by a parable I was once told. There was a stone in the corner of a meadow and under that stone lived a colony of ants. They were just ordinary ants but among them lived a genius ant, an Einstein ant. One day the board of the colony addressed the genius ant, telling it that there was nothing more for it to learn and it would have to leave them and go out into the world. So on a misty October evening the colony bestowed its valediction on the genius and it made its entry into the world. There happened to be a totally non-metaphysical horse grazing nearby. Regardless of how brilliant our genius ant is, it will never be able to perceive the horse, such is the disproportion in size. . . . So I wonder are there presences all around us, that because of the disproportion between our senses and their presence, we are not picking up at all? We are seeing a lot more vacancy and voids in the world than actually exist. Maybe it is the role of the artists and mystics to attend to the seeming emptiness about us and find incredible riches there. Wendell Berry is one such artist. He is a farmer and writer who lives in Kentucky and he attends deeply to nature. I will conclude with a beautiful poem of his from the series *Sabbaths,* entitled "I Go Among Trees and Sit Still."

I Go Among Trees and Sit Still

I go among trees and sit still
All my stirring becomes quiet around me like
circles on water,
My tasks lie in their places where I left them,
asleep like cattle,
Then what is afraid of me comes and lives
awhile in my sight,
What it fears in me leaves me and the fear of me
leaves it,
It sings and I hear its song,
Then what I am afraid of comes,
I live for a while in its sight
What I fear in it leaves it, and the fear of it
leaves me.

It sings and I hear its song
After days of labor, mute in my consternations
I hear my song at last, and I sing it.
As we sing, the day turns, the trees move.

In Praise of the Earth

Let us bless
The imagination of the Earth.
That knew early the patience
To harness the mind of time,
Waited for the seas to warm,
Ready to welcome the emergence
Of things dreaming of voyaging
Among the stillness of land.

And how light knew to nurse
The growth until the face of the earth
Brightens beneath a vision of color

When the ages of ice came
And sealed the earth inside
An endless coma of cold,
The heart of the earth held hope,
Storing fragments of memory,
Ready for the return of the sun.

Let us thank the Earth
That offers ground for home
And holds our feet firm
To walk in space open
To infinite galaxies.

Let us salute the silence,
And certainty of mountains:
Their sublime stillness,
Their dream-filled hearts.

The wonder of a garden
Trusting the first warmth of spring
Until its black infinity of cells
Becomes charged with dream;
Then the silent, slow nurture
Of the seed's self, coaxing it
To trust the act of death.

The humility of the earth
That transfigures all
That has fallen
Of outlived growth.

The kindness of the earth,
Opening to receive
Our worn forms
Into the final stillness.

Let us ask forgiveness of the earth
For all our sins against her:
For our violence and poisonings
Of her beauty.

Let us remember within us
The ancient clay,
Holding the memory of seasons,
The passion of the wind,
The fluency of water,
The warmth of fire,
The quiver-touch of the sun
And shadowed sureness of the moon.

That we may awaken,
To live to the full
The dream of the earth
Who chose us to emerge
And incarnate its hidden night
In mind, spirit and light.

From *To Bless the Space Between Us*

ABSENCE

"While we are here in the world, where
is it that we are absent from?"

I produced "The Open Mind" for RTÉ Radio
from 1989 to 2002. Each year we featured
"The Open Mind Guest Lecture"—a talk
given before an invited audience in the Radio
Centre, RTÉ, by a guest speaker. Speakers over the years included Gordon Wilson,
Michael D. Higgins, Erskine Childers, John
Hume, Anne Fine and George Mitchell. The
subjects varied from Northern Ireland to
children's books. In 1997, I invited John to
give the lecture and he chose as his topic—
"Towards a Philosophy of Absence."

ABSENCE IS SOMETHING THAT I HAVE THOUGHT about for a long time. It is a beautiful theme. There seems to be very little written on it, and the more I thought about it, the more I became aware of how many dimensions of our lives it actually touches. I would like to begin the lecture by trying to locate the first experience of absence in some primal kind of moment.

When each of us was born, we became present to the earth and we entered into an ancient narrative of presence that preceded us by hundreds and thousands of millions of years. I think that the first experience that the earth had of real absence was when the human mind first emerged. That must have been an amazing experience for the actual earth itself. It had, up to then, created incredible masterpieces. If you ever see a twilight, with the incredible nuance and depth of color that it has; if you look at the amazing choruses of waves that beat against a shoreline; if you look at the mystical shape of mountains, the voice of streams and rivers and the undomesticable wildness of certain wilderness places, you will know that the imagination of the earth had created great beauty.

ABSENCE AND LOSS

I think that absence is the sister of presence; the opposite of presence is not absence, but vacancy. Vacancy is a neutral, indifferent, inane, blank kind of space, whereas absence has real energy; it has vitality in it, and it is infused with longing. Sometimes a great way to come to know a word is to go back to its roots. If you go back to the roots of the word "absence," you find that it is rooted in Latin, *ab esse*—to be elsewhere. To be absent is to be away from a person, or a place; it is an act of departure from your expected and natural belonging. So all absence holds the echo of some fractured intimacy, but the intimacy came first, and then, when it was broken, the absence filled the heart. The most common experience of absence is when you lose a friend who is close to you. This indicates the regions of absence that people every human life. When you open yourself to the activity and sacrament of friendship with someone, you create a unique and particular kind of space with them; a special space that you share in the same way with no one else. And when the friend departs— when a relationship breaks or when you lose someone in that final severance that we call death—absence haunts your heart and makes your belonging sore and painful. In some way, there is still within you some kind of innocence that is either unable or unwilling to accept that the person has finally gone and forever. So absence is never clear-cut. Everyone that leaves your life leaves a subtle trail of connection with you; and when you think of them, and miss them and desire them, your heart journeys out again along that trail towards them in the elsewhere that they now find themselves.

Physically considered, we are all objects; we are physical, bodily objects. But considered in terms of affection, effectively, there are myriad secret pathways that go out from every heart. They go out to the earth, they go out to intimate places, they go out to the past. And they go out particularly towards the friends that are really close to us.

MIDHIR AND ÉTAÍN

When I was preparing this talk, I was looking back along the old tradition to see if there were any ancient Irish stories about absence, and I came upon the beautiful legend of Midhir and Étaín. The fairy prince Midhir fell in love with Étaín, and Midhir's wife, Fuamnach, was very jealous, so, with the help of a druid, she changed Étaín into a butterfly, and then, to add more fury, she set a terrible storm going, which blew Étaín all through the country for seven years, until she finally landed at the palace of Aengus, the god of love. He recognized her even though she was a butterfly, took her in, built invisible walls around her, and gave her a beautiful garden. During the night, she came back to the form of a woman, and during the day she was a butterfly. But Fuamnach found out about it and chased her again with a storm, until she landed again in another palace and fell into the goblet of the queen as she was drinking wine. The queen drank her down, and she was reborn nine months later as a beautiful child, whom they, unknowingly, called Étaín again. All the time, the lover Midhir longed for her, searched every corner of the country, and could not find her. Then she grew up to be a beautiful woman, and the king of Tara, the High King of Ireland, took her as his wife.

One day, at the great gathering—the great assembly in Tara—Midhir recognized her as the one his heart had so hungered for and whose absence had haunted him. He invited her to go back to him, but she did not recognize him because her last metamorphosis had erased her memory completely. He then played the king in a game of chess and he won. He asked that, for his winning, he be allowed to receive one kiss from Étaín. He met her, and when she heard that—the king didn't let him kiss her for a long time!—some knowing within her was kindled again, and she began to dream of her former life. Little by little, she began to recall all that she had forgotten and, as she did, her love for Midhir returned totally. When he came back to kiss her, the king had an army around not to let him in, but magically he appeared in the middle of the assembly hall and embraced her. The king came to attack them and they weren't there. When the king's men went outside, they looked up and there were two white swans circling in the starry heavens above the palace.

It is a beautiful story to show how, when love or friendship happens, a distinctively unique tone is struck, a unique space is created, and the loss of this is a haunting absence. The faithfulness of the absence kept Midhir on the quest until he eventually rediscovered her, awoke the absence in her again, and then the two of them became present as swans, ironically in the air element that had created the distance and had created the torture for her.

I believe that the death of every animal and every person creates a kind of an invisible ruin in the world, and that, as the world gets older, it becomes more full with these invisible ruins of vanished presence. Emily Dickinson puts it beautifully when she says:

Absence disembodies—so does Death
hiding individuals from the Earth

It is exactly that act of hiding that causes absence. We
are so vulnerable to absence because we desire presence so
deeply.

PRESENCE

One of the deepest longings of the human heart is for
real presence. Real presence is the goal of truth, the ideal
of love and the intentionality of prayer here and in the
beatific vision in the hereafter. Real presence is the heart
of the incarnation and it is also the heart of the Eucharist.
This is where imagination works so beautifully with the
absences and emptiness of life. It always tries to find a
shape of words or music or color or stone that will in some
way incarnate new presence to fill the absence. I remember once in Venice, during an amazing music festival, I
attended an outdoor concert in Piazza San Marco, with
Stravinsky's music and a ballet, and the moon was full
and the sea was wild. There were certain moments in that
concert when moon and ocean and dance and music and
audience congealed into one pulse—an amazing experience of unity, and, in some strange way, a breakthrough

to real presence. When we experience real presence, we break through to that which is latently in us, that is eternal, but which the normal daily round of life keeps distant from us.

ALIENATION

The social world is usually governed by a sophisticated and very intricate grammar of absence. You think of the work you do and the people you work with. You think of people who do work that you wouldn't like, people who have to hit the one bolt every twenty seconds for a full day. There is no way that you could do that, unless, of course, you were a saint or a Zen mystic, with real intention. The only way you can do it is by somehow being in conditioned reflex and being actually absent and away elsewhere. That is what I think Karl Marx had in mind when he talked about alienation; in some sense there are certain kinds of functions which diminish and empty our own self-presence and make us absent to our own lives. To do these things continuously in this divided way brings us far away from who we are and from what we are called to do here. That is *real* alienation.

WELCOME ABSENCE

Of course, sometimes it is lovely to be absent from things. I am reminded of a writer who, in describing a character, said, "He has quite a good presence, but a perfectly delightful absence!" In other words, when he wasn't around, happiness increased in some way. There's a lovely Palestinian American poet that I like, called Naomi Shihab Nye, who has a wonderful poem called "The Art of Disappearing" that I would like to read.

> When they say, "Don't I know you?"
> say "No."
>
> When they invite you to a party,
> remember what parties are like
> before answering.
> Someone telling you in a loud voice
> they once wrote a poem.
> Greasy sausage balls on a paper plate.
>
> Then reply.
>
> If they say, "We should get together,"
> say, "Why?"
> It's not that you don't love them anymore.
> You're trying to remember something

too important to forget.
Trees. The monastery bell at twilight.

Tell them you have a new project.
It will never be finished.

When someone recognizes you in a grocery
store,
nod briefly and become a cabbage.
When someone you haven't seen in ten years
appears at the door,
don't start singing him all your new songs.
You will never catch up.

Walk around feeling like a leaf.
Know you could tumble any second.
Then decide what to do with your time.

The art of disappearing certainly has its own kind of value. In a strange way, in modern society we seem to be inhabiting the world of absence more than presence through the whole world of technology and virtual reality. Very often it seems that the driven nature of contemporary society is turning us into the ultimate harvesters of absence, that is, ghosts in our own lives.

In post-modern culture, the mind is particularly homeless, haunted by a sense of absence that it can neither understand nor transfigure. Many of the traditional shelters have fallen down. Religion seems more and more, certainly in its official presentation, to speak in an idiom that is unable to converse with the modern spiritual hunger. Politics seems devoid of vision and is becoming more and more synonymous with economics. Consumerist culture worships accumulation and power, and creates, with incredible arrogance, its own hollow and gaudy hierarchies. In this country, in our admiration for the achievement and velocity of the Celtic Tiger, we are refusing to notice the paw-marks of its ravages and the unglamorous remains of its prey.

FALSE ABSENCE

Our time is often filled up with forced presence, every minute filled out with something, but every minute merely an instant, lacking the patience and mystery of continuity that awakens that which is eternal within time. Sometimes, when people in a society are unable to read or decipher the labyrinth of absence, their homeless minds revert to nostalgia. They see the present as a massive fall from a once glorious past, where perfect morality, pure faith and impeccable family values pertained, without critique or alternative or any smudge of complexity or unhappiness. All fundamentalism is based both on faulty perception and on unreal nostalgia. What is created is a fake absence in relation to the past. It is used to look away from the challenge and potential of the present and to create a future which is meant to resemble a past that never actually existed. It is very sad, sometimes, to see the way a grid of a certain kind of language can form over a person's spirit and hold them completely trapped and transfixed in a very stiff ideological position. It happens an awful lot in religion. Sometimes, a grid of dead religious language blocks the natural pores of people's spirit. Blind faith is meant to be ultimate sanctity, but it is merely an exercise in absence that keeps you away from that which is truly your own and keeps you outside the magic and playfulness and dangerous otherness of divinity.

As we journey onwards in our lives, we seem to accumulate more and more absences. This is very marked in relation to old people; their most intimate friends are usually in the unseen world among the dead. But any life that is vigorous and open to challenge and compassion and the real activity of thought knows that, as we journey, we create many tabernacles of absence within us.

MEMORY

Yet, there is a place where our vanished days secretly gather. Memory, as a kingdom, is full of the ruins of presence. It is fascinating that, in your memory, nothing is lost or ever finally forgotten. We all have had experience of this. Sometimes the needle of thought finds its way into a groove of memory and suddenly an old experience that you no longer remembered comes back almost pure and fresh and intact to you. So memory is the place where absence is transfigured and where our time in the world is secretly held for us. As we grow older, our bodies diminish, but our minds and our memories grow more intense. Yet our culture is very amnesiac. And amnesia is an incredible thing. Imagine if—God between us and all harm—you had an accident and you lost your memory completely. You wouldn't know who you were, where you were or who you were with. So, in a certain sense, memory keeps presence alive and is always bringing out of what seemed to be absent new forms of presence.

THE UNKNOWN

There is another level of absence as well, and it is that which has not vanished, but that which has not yet arrived. We all live in a pathway in the middle of time, so there are lots of events, people, places, thoughts, experiences still ahead of us that have not actually arrived at the door of our hearts at all. This is the world of the unknown. Questions and thinking are ways of reaching into the unknown to find out what kind of treasures it actually holds. The question is the place where the unknown becomes articulate in us. A good question is something that has incredible grace and light and depth to it. A good question is something that always, in some way, plows the invisible furrows of absence to find the nourishment and the treasure that we actually need.

IMAGINATION

This is where the imagination plays a powerful role, because the imagination loves absence rather than presence. Absence is full of possibility and it always brings us back new reports from the unknown that is yet to come towards us. This is especially true in art. Music is the art form that most perfectly sculpts and draws out the poignance of the silence between the notes. Really good music has an incredible secret sculpture of silence in it. The wonderful conductor who died several months ago, Georg Solti, said that, towards the end of his life, he was becoming ever more fascinated with the secret presence of silence within music. If you listen to Mozart's Requiem, or Wagner's overture to *Tristan and Isolde,* you will know the beauty and poignance of absence as expressed in music. Then, if you want to go for something totally different, that amazing man Lou Reed recorded an incredible album a few years ago—an album of tormented hymns to two close friends of his who died. It is called *Magic and Loss,* and there you will see absence in an incredibly intense and powerful kind of way.

The imagination is always fascinated by what is absent. The first time you read a short story, it is very frustrating, because the best story is the one that is not told at all. The short story will bring you to a threshold and leave you there, and you will be dying to know what happened to the character, or how did the story go further. It is not cheating you—it is bringing you to a threshold and inviting you to open the door for yourself, so that you can have a genuinely original and new experience. So the imagination always recognizes that the most enthralling aspect of presence is actually that which is omitted. The art of writing a really good poem is to know what to leave out. John McGahern said that, when he has finished a manuscript, he goes back over it and the first pieces that he starts doing surgery on are the pieces he likes best! He knows that these are the pieces that he can't trust himself with. You gradually sculpt the thing back until you have a slender shape which has lots of holes in it, but in this absence, you give free play to the imagination to fill it out for itself. You respect the dignity and potential of the reader.

The imagination is incredibly important in this respect in contemporary society, because it mirrors the complexity of our souls. Society always reduces everything to a simple common denominator; religion does it, politics does it, the media does it as well. Only the imagination has the willingness to witness that which is really complex, dark, paradoxical, contradictory and awkward within us, that which doesn't fit comfortably on the veneer of the social surface. So we depend on the imagination to trawl and retrieve our poignant and wounded complexity which has to remain absent from the social surface. The imagination is really the inspired and uncautious priestess who, against the wishes of all systems and structures, insists on celebrating the liturgy of presence at the banished altars of absence. So the imagination is faithful to the full home of the heart, and all its rooms.

Often in country places—probably in the city too—there was a haunted house, which no one would go into and people would pass with great care, especially late at night. I often think that there is, in every life, some haunted room that you never want to go into, and that you do your best to forget was there at all. You will never break in that door with your mind, or with your will. Only with the gentle coaxing of the imagination will that door be opened to you and will you be given the gift back again of a part of yourself that either you or someone else had forced you to drive away and reject.

If you look at the characters in literature, there are no saints, because saints, in terms of the imagination, are not interesting people. They are too good. The imagination is always interested in where things break down—failure, resentment, defeat, contradiction, bitterness, darkness, glory, light and possibility—the wild side of ourselves that society would rather forget was there at all. So the imagination mirrors and articulates also that constant companion dimension of the heart that, by definition and design, remains perennially absent—the subconscious. All we know of ourselves is just a certain little surface and there is a whole under-earth of complexity to us that, by definition, keeps out of our sight. It is actually absent to us. It comes through dreams. Sometimes it comes very powerfully through crises or through trauma, but the imagination is the presence within us that brings that hidden, netted grounding side of ourselves up to the surface, and can coax it into harmony with our daily self that we actually know. It is amazing how many of your needs and hungers and potential and gifts and blindness are actually rooted in the subconscious side of your life, and most of that great plantation of your subconscious seems to have actually happened in the playfields and innocence of childhood.

Childhood is an amazing forest of mystery. One of the sad things about contemporary society is the way that childhood has been shrunk back and children now only have a few years of natural innocence before the force and metallic and sophistication of the world is actually in on top of them. It frightens me sometimes to think of the effect this might have on them later on in their lives. One of the great things that keeps failure, resentment, defeat, contradiction, bitterness at bay is the great forest of your childhood that holds everything anchored there for you.

MEDIA ABSENCE

Now, to relate this to the social level, absence works very powerfully here; in other words, media represent society—they are the mirror of society in a way; they have a powerful, coloring influence on the thin and rapid stream of public perception. And yet media are not straight or direct; they are always involved in the act of selectivity—who appears on the news, how is the news structured? And who are the people in our society that we never see? Who are the absent ones that we never hear from? There are many of them, and, when you start thinking about it, they are usually the poor and the vulnerable. We have no idea, those of us who are privileged, of the conditions in which so many poor and underprivileged people actually live. Because it is not our world, we don't actually see it at all. So these people are absent and they are deliberately kept out, because their voices are awkward, they are uncomfortable, and they make us feel very uneasy.

ILLNESS

Another kind of absence in life that is very frightening is the sudden absence of health; when illness arrives. Your self-belonging can no longer be spontaneous and you are now invited, in serious illness, to live in a bleak world that you don't know. You have to negotiate and work everything as if you are starting a new kind of life. Those who are mentally insane live in a jungle of symbols where there is only the smallest order, and sometimes, when there are clearings there, and when they see how haunted they are, there must be a feeling and an experience of such awful poignance.

IMPRISONMENT

Then there are those who are sentenced to be absent from their homes, and from their lives, and these are the prisoners. One of the fears that I always had—even as a child—was the fear that you could be arrested for something that you never did, but that you could never prove that you hadn't actually done it. I have known friends of mine who went to jail for different things, and the force of anonymity that is brought down to unravel your presence and your identity is just unbelievable. There are people who have done awful things, and of course we have to put them away, but the actual experience of prisoners must be terrible. It must be terrible to be living thirty years of your life in Mountjoy jail. Your one life on the earth. Joseph Brodsky, who was in jail, said, "The awful thing about being a prisoner and being in jail is that you have very limited space, and unlimited time." When you put those two things together, it is an incredible load on the mind.

EMIGRATION

The other aspect of absence that I'd like to mention in an Irish context is the absence of Irish people from their own country; the massive hemorrhage of emigration that has been happening over decades and over centuries. I remember working in America when I was about nineteen or twenty, meeting an old man from our village at home. He was about eighty-five years of age and had left when he was eighteen and had never gone back. Even though he was physically in America, in his mind he was still in north Clare. He could remember the names of fields, pathways, stones, trees in camera-precise detail. It must be a wrenching thing to have to be absent from your own place in a totally different kind of world. This raises all kinds of economic and political questions.

CONTEMPLATIVES

Then there are those who deliberately choose the way of absence. These are the contemplatives. They are amazing people; they leave behind the whole bustle of the world, and submit their vulnerable minds to the acidic solitude of the contemplative cell. They are called to face outside social absence and the labyrinths of inner absence, and who knows how they civilize and warm the bleak territories of loss and emptiness for the rest of us? I am sure that if you could read the actual soul or psychic arithmetic of the world, it is unknown what evil and destruction and darkness such contemplative prayer transfigures and keeps away from us. Noel Dermot O'Donoghue, the wonderful Carmelite mystic from the kingdom of Kerry, says that the contemplatives or the mystics are people who withdraw from the world to confront the monster in its lair. Maybe our tranquillity is an unknown gift from all those unglamorous absent ones who are called or forced to excavate the salt mines of absence. I also think that people who are ill, and who carry illness for decades in rooms that no one goes into—it is unknown the mystical creativity of the work that they actually do.

ABSENCE OF GOD

And finally, to come on to one of the great absences from the world, which everyone complains about, and that is the absence of God. Particularly in our century, with the Holocaust and the world wars, Yugoslavia and all the rest of it, there's a great cry out against the absence of God. In the eighteenth century, Hegel said God was dead, and then in the nineteenth century, Nietzsche took that up; it is an old question. In the classical tradition, theologians were aware of the absence of God as well. There was the notion of the *Deus absconditus,* the absconded or vanished God. One of the points of absolute subversive realism of the Christian story is that Christ came out of the safety of the sky and stood in Calvary against the absolute silence of God and carried the suffering of the world. The Crucifixion is that bleak place where no certainty can ever settle, and the realism of that is incredibly truthful to the depth and power of absence that suffering and pain and oppression bring to the world. And that is what the Eucharist is about; in the Eucharist you have the most amazing symphony of complete presence based on the ultimate absence and the ultimate kind of emptiness. It is fascinating, too, that sometimes absence creates new possibility. When the carpenter rose from the dead, they wanted him to stay around, and he said no, that he must go, in order

to let the Spirit come. So sometimes that which is absent
allows something new to emerge.

DEATH

The final absence I want to deal with is the absence that
none of us will be finally able to avoid—your own absence
from the earth, and that will happen to us in death. Death
is the ultimate absence. Part of the sadness of contemporary
society that has lost its mystical and mythological webbing
is that we can no longer converse with the dead, and we are
no longer aware of them. The dead are notoriously absent
from us. I think that you can characterize your life in different ways. One of the ways is the time before someone
that is close to you dies, and the time afterwards. That
happened for me when my uncle died. I would like to read
this poem, called "November Questions," where I tried to
trawl the vacancy of his absence for some little glimpse or
signal of who he was now, or where he was.

November Questions

Where did you go
when your eyes closed

and you were cloaked
in the ancient cold?

How did we seem,
huddled around
the hospital bed?
Did we loom as
figures do in dream?

As your skin drained,
became vellum,
a splinter of whitethorn
from your battle with a bush
in the Seangharraí
stood out in your thumb.

Did your new feet
take you beyond
to fields of Elysia
or did you come back
along Caherbeanna mountain
where every rock
knows your step?

Did you have to go
to a place unknown?

Were there friendly faces
to welcome you,
help you settle in?

Did you recognize anyone?

Did it take long
to lose
the web of scent,
the honey smell of old hay,
the whiff of wild mint
and the wet odor of the earth
you turned every spring?

Did sounds become
unlinked,
the bellow of cows
let into fresh winterage
the purr of a stray breeze
over the Coillín,
the ring of the galvanized bucket
that fed the hens,
the clink of limestone
loose over a scailp
in the Ciorcán?

Did you miss
the delight of your gaze
at the end of a day's work
over a black garden,
a new wall
or a field cleared of rock?

Have you someone there
that you can talk to,
someone who is drawn
to the life you carry?

With your new eyes
can you see from within?
Is it we who seem
outside?

From *Echoes of Memory*

There is one force that pervades both presence and absence, cannot be located particularly anywhere, and can be subtracted from nowhere, and that force is spirit. We talk of absence and space, and absence and time, but we can never talk about the absence of spirit, because spirit, by nature and definition, can never be absent. So, all space is spiritual space, and in spiritual space there is no real distance. And this raises the question I would like to end with—a fascinating question: while we are here in the world, where is it that we are absent from?

For Absence

May you know that absence is alive within hidden
    presence, that nothing is ever lost or forgotten.

May the absences in your life grow full of eternal
    echo.

May you sense around you the secret Elsewhere
    where the presences that have left you dwell.

May you be generous in your embrace of loss.

May the sore well of grief turn into a seamless flow
    of presence.

May your compassion reach out to the ones we never
    hear from.

May you have the courage to speak for the excluded
    ones.

May you become the gracious and passionate subject
   of your own life.

May you not disrespect your mystery through brittle
   words or false belonging.

May you be embraced by God in whom dawn and
   twilight are one.

May your longing inhabit its dreams within the
   Great Belonging.

From *To Bless the Space Between Us*

DAWN MASS

"There are limitless possibilities within each one
of us and, if we give ourselves any chance at
all, it is unknown what we are capable of."

In the early 1990s John initiated the idea
of a Dawn Mass on Easter Sunday—a
practice that has since grown in popularity
across the country. He chose a very special
and sacred site—the magnificent ruined
abbey of Corcomroe in the heart of the Burren, Co. Clare. The abbey was built by the
Cistercians in the eleventh/twelfth centuries. It was quite an extraordinary sight to
see a procession of cars snaking along Burren roads to the abbey in the dark of the

night (around 5 a.m.). The Dawn Mass was very much a community effort, as the local parishioners prepared an altar in the cemetery surrounding the abbey with a huge paschal fire nearby. They marshaled the traffic. Local musicians provided traditional airs throughout the ceremony. And there were tea and buns for everyone at the end of Mass. Hundreds of people have converged on the abbey. What follows is taken from a recording made on Easter Sunday, April 15, 1992. The light of the paschal fire pierces the dark and the first twitterings of the dawn chorus are heard as John begins . . .

IN THE NAME OF THE FATHER, AND THE SON and the Holy Spirit.

I would like to welcome you all to Corcomroe to celebrate the Resurrection.

First of all, I would remind you that we are in a very sacred place—a Cistercian monastery going back to the eleventh/twelfth century—and we are here not to disturb those who are buried here nor the spirits of those who lived and prayed here for centuries. We are here to bring the light of the Resurrection and of the dawn. We begin in the darkness of night, with the beautiful light of the Burren moon gradually bringing the shapes of the mountains into view. So just for a few minutes we'll have a slow air to concentrate our attention and focus on what we are here to do.

Music

At the beginning of the Eucharist, let us realize that there is a special gift of light and healing in this holy place for each of us on this Easter morning. For a moment in silence, let us call to mind the areas of our lives where we particularly need Easter light and healing and hope . . .

Silence

And let us ask first of all for healing for our sins of fear, for the areas where we are afraid in our hearts and spirits and where we haven't the courage to enter fully the lives that God has so generously given us—

Lord have mercy.

People: Lord have mercy

And let us ask forgiveness for any sins of blindness that we have—blindness to the opportunities that we have to grow and be creative and that we indirectly reject—

Christ have mercy.

People: Christ have mercy

Let us ask forgiveness for any sins of resentment or bitterness, which put our lives out of joint and take the peace and natural courage that we are supposed to have—
Lord have mercy.

People: Lord have mercy

Let us ask forgiveness for any wrong we have done to anyone, directly in word or deed or indirectly through bad mind or any kind of negativity—
Lord have mercy.

People: Lord have mercy

Let us ask on this Easter morning that all the frailty of our minds and spirits may be healed and that we be given the healing and courage for a new beginning on our journey through life—
Lord have mercy.

People: Lord have mercy

Dawn Mass

And now as the dawn light approaches, we have an old Irish air as a *Gloria* celebration.

Music

Let us pray.

Lord, you have given us the gift of this new dawn, the dawn on which Jesus rose from the dead and broke, finally and forever, the chains of darkness and blindness. We ask that streams of Easter light might flow into the intimacy and privacy of our hearts this morning, to heal us and encourage us and enable each of us to make again a new beginning. We ask this through Christ our Lord.

People: Amen.

First Reading from the Acts of the Apostles (10:37–43)

Music

Second Reading from First Letter of St. Paul

to the Corinthians (5:6–8)

Gospel from St. John (20:1–9)

Music

HOMILY

We are always on our way from darkness into light. Every morning, we come out of the dark territories of dreaming into waking awareness of the day. Every night, no matter how long, breaks again and the light of dawn comes. At birth each of us made a journey from darkness into light, from the warm secure darkness of the womb into the light of the world. So we are no strangers to darkness and we are special friends of the light. A human life is guided, balanced and poised by the light of the mind and spirit of the person. In the darkness of our bodies, and particularly of our brains, the light of the mind is attuned and alive. There are great primal thresholds in life, and one of the most beautiful and most encouraging and most healing is the threshold of dawn, when darkness gives way to the light and novelty and wonder of a new day. Days are where we live our lives, where everything happens to us. It's lovely to think that at the heart of our belief in God, there is a young man, a carpenter from a small town, who braved in an extreme way the darkness of the human journey and took upon his tender shoulders, in a most brutal and harrowing way, all darkness everywhere. He took it to the summit of Calvary, where that darkness was turned into a light that never quenched.

Here in north Clare there is the tradition of winterage, where cattle are put out for new grazing. In doing this, some people went astray in the night and "Jack O'Lantern" was blamed for this. Old people will tell you that the way to break this spell was to turn your coat inside out. On Resurrection morning the dark and lonesome cross was turned inside out. When the cross hits your life, a loneliness, a blindness and a darkness come all around you. Darkness and lostness are the worst parts of suffering. The wonder of the Resurrection is that this darkness was opened out and at the heart of the darkness a secret light was discovered. Each one of us who has come here hasn't come to this place out of curiosity but we have come because we know the need that is in our lives and we know the frailty that is in our hearts and minds. We are strangers in the world. In our journey through life anything can befall us. It seems to be very difficult for us as humans to learn how to love, to learn how to let the fear and the resentment and the blindness fall away from us and to come into the special joy and peace and freedom of love. No matter how assured or competent we may feel, there is none of us who has not large territories of fear in our hearts, fear of sharing ourselves, of opening ourselves, of entering life. That is why we come to an ancient holy place like this, before the dawn, to let the new tender light of the Resurrection touch our helpless fear and transfigure it and open it into courage. We come here also because we have all been hurt in our lives. One of the beauties of Easter morning is that the light that comes with Christ is a gentle but penetrating light. There is no hurt anywhere within us, no matter in what crevices it might be buried, but that the light of this Easter can reach it and heal it.

To be born is to be chosen. None of us is accidentally in the world. We are sent here because there is something special for each of us to do here that could not be done by someone else. One of the wisdoms of living a full life is to try and sense what it is you were sent here for and to try and let the hindrances that block you from that fall away so that you can claim completely the life that was so generously offered to you. We were all reared in a world that concentrated on sin and sinfulness, but I believe that when we come into the eternal world we won't so much be checked for our failures, but we will be asked whether we honored the possibilities that were placed inside us when we were so carefully fashioned out of the clay. There are limitless possibilities within each one of us and, if we give ourselves any chance at all, it is unknown what we are capable of. So on this Easter morning, let us look again at the lives we have been so generously given and let us let fall away the useless baggage that we carry—old pains, old habits, old ways of seeing and feeling—and let us have the courage to begin again. Life is very short, and we are no sooner here than it is time to depart again, and we should use to the full the time that we still have.

We don't realize all the good we can do. A kind, encouraging word or a helping hand can bring many a person through dark valleys in their lives. We weren't put here to make money or to acquire status or reputation. We were sent here to search for the light of Easter in our hearts, and when we find it we are meant to give it away generously. The dawn that is rising this Easter morning is a gift to our hearts and we are meant to celebrate it and to carry away from this holy, ancient place the gifts of healing and light and the courage of a new beginning.

Silent Reflection

BLESSING OF THE ELEMENTS

Air: One of the oldest words in Greek is the word for "air"—*pneuma*—and it is also the word for "spirit." One of the first words for God in Hebrew is *Rua,* which also means "wind." Bless the air we breathe, Lord. Let us close our eyes and breathe in the fresh air of this dawn and then breathe out the darkness that is within us and inhibiting us.

Silence

Earth: Our bodies are made of the earth, and at the end of our lives will return to the earth. We ask forgiveness of Mother Earth for all the ways we have abused and poisoned and destroyed her. We put our hand to the ground and ask the earth to heal us and bless us.

Fire: Fire is the great cleanser and purifier. We ask that this fire of Easter may burn away from our hearts all that is false and useless and negative inside us.

Water: Water is the gift of life, and without it there is

no life. We thank God for the gift of water and ask him to bless with Easter light this water taken from the ocean surrounding us, and in receiving it may we be cleansed and blessed, that we may be protected from all danger and darkness, so that the spirit of evil may have no power over us or those that are close to us among the living and the dead.

PRAYERS OF THE FAITHFUL

That the light of Easter may fully enter our hearts and change us and bless us.

Lord, hear us
Lord, graciously hear us

For all those that we love, and especially for the gift of friendship, and that our friends may be blessed with the same kindness and generosity which they show us.

Lord, hear us
Lord, graciously hear us

For those who are suffering in the world. For those in hospital, that God might bless them and that the light of Easter might surprise them and give them courage. For those who are depressed and for those who are haunted and locked away in institutions, that they too may receive the special peace of Easter. For prisoners everywhere, that though they have lost the outside world, the gifts of the inner world might be opened up to them. For those who suffer injustice in the world, those starving to death in a world where there is too much food—and that we may be forgiven for our guilt in participating in systems that cause suffering to others.

Lord, hear us
Lord, graciously hear us

For all the people of this parish, especially those who are ill or who have died in the past year. And for all our own particular intentions.

Lord, hear us
Lord, graciously hear us

Lord, you know the deepest needs of our hearts. We ask you to renew us and transform us in the new dawn light of Easter.

Amen.

Music
Priest and congregation move inside the ruined
abbey for the Consecration of the Mass. At the
end of Mass, John gives the final blessing.

May the spirit and light of this Easter morning and the special spirit and light of this abbey of Corcomroe bless us all, watch over us and protect us on our journey and open us from the darkness into the light of peace and hope and transfiguration. May the spirit of the sacred Trinity, the light of nature and all good spirits and angels and our friends among the dead bless us and heal us, the Father, the Son and the Holy Spirit.

Amen

This Mass is ended, but don't go yet because there's tea and buns outside and a feast of reels to send us home happy!

A Morning Offering

I bless the night that nourished my heart
To set the ghosts of longing free
Into the flow and figure of dream

That went to harvest from the dark
Bread for the hunger no one sees.

All that is eternal in me
Welcomes the wonder of this day,
The field of brightness it creates
Offering time for each thing
To arise and illuminate.

I place on the altar of dawn:
The quiet loyalty of breath,
The tent of thought where I shelter
And all beauty drawn to the eye.

May my mind come alive today
To the invisible geography
That invites me to new frontiers,
To break the dead shell of yesterdays,
To risk being disturbed and changed.

May I have the courage today
To live the life that I would love,
To postpone my dream no longer,
But do at last what I came here for
And waste my heart on fear no more.

From *To Bless the Space Between Us*

BALANCE

"Most of us are moving through such an undergrowth of excess that we cannot sense the shape of ourselves anymore."

Between 1998 and 2010, the Céifin Institute (largely under the driving force of Fr. Harry Bohan) held a series of annual conferences in Ennis, Co. Clare. They took a hard look at "our society in the new millennium," beginning with the prescient question "Are we forgetting something?" (I.e., in the midst of an economic boom, what has happened to our values?) These were stimulating and challenging events, addressed by high-powered speakers from home and abroad. For me as a broadcaster they were the source of many lively contributions to "The Open Mind," in either interview or extract form. The theme for 1999 was "Working Towards Balance" and John O'Donohue was a guest speaker who undertook his own exploration of "Balance." As an introduction to his talk, John read his poem "Thought-Work," in which the working of the mind is compared to the work of the architect-crows he observed building their nests in the Burren.

Thought-Work

Off course from the frail music sought by words
And the path that always claims the journey,
In the pursuit of a more oblique rhythm,
Creating mostly its own geography,
The mind is an old crow
Who knows only to gather dead twigs,
Then take them back to the vacancy
Between the branches of the parent tree
And entwine them around the emptiness
With silence and unfailing patience

Until what was fallen, withered and lost
Is now set to fill with dreams as a nest.

From *Conamara Blues*

AN EXPLORATION OF BALANCE

The Concept of Balance in a Theory of Creation

One of my favorite sentences in the Western philosophical tradition is from Leibniz; it was subsequently used by Schelling and Heidegger: "The real mystery is not that things are the way they are, but that there is *something* rather than nothing." I think this is a great sentence, because it alerts one immediately to the mystery of the presence of things, which we so often tend to forget. In post-modern culture, we live increasingly in a virtual world and seem to have lost visceral and vital contact with the actual world.

Another way of looking at this statement is: the real mystery is that there is so much. Everywhere the human eye looks, everywhere the human mind turns, there is a huge panorama of diversity; the difference that lives in everything and between everything, the fact that no two stones, no two fields, no two faces or no two biographies are the same. The range and intensity of this difference is quite staggering. This is not an abstract thing. People who live in small farms in country areas could spend hours telling you about all the differences they experience between two places in the same field. Patrick Kavanagh spoke of the "undying difference in the corner of a field."

The difference that inhabits experience and the world is not raw chaos; it has a certain structure. It is quite amazing to consider the hidden, implicit structures that exist in all the natural things. For instance, the way water falls so elegantly, always with structure. Even the water from the tires of a car as it goes down a highway or street can have a beautiful structure. There is huge differentiation in the world, and its structure often seems to be one of duality; in other words, two sides of the one object or reality.

If you reflect on your own experience, you will see that you are already familiar with duality. There is light and darkness, beginning and ending, inside and outside, above and below, masculine and feminine, divine and human, time and eternity, soul and sense, word and silence. The really fascinating thing is not that these dualities are there, but the threshold where they actually meet each other. I believe that any notion of balance that is really authentic has to work with the notion of threshold. Otherwise, balance is just a functional strategy without any ontological depth or grounding. In the Western tradition, that line, that threshold between light and darkness, between soul and body, God and human, between ourselves and nature has often been atrophied. When the threshold freezes, the two sides get cut off from each other and the result is dualism. That kind of separation has really blighted and damaged the Western tradition. You can see this in very simple ways. For instance, in Catholic Ireland there was a division between the soul and the senses. The senses were supposed to be bad, and the body pulled you down, whereas the soul wanted to bring you up. That split caused untold guilt and pain for people.

Duality, then, is informed by the oppositions that meet at this threshold. I would argue that an authentic life is a life that is aware of and willing to engage its own oppositions, and honorably inhabits that threshold where the light and darkness, the masculine and feminine and all the beginnings and endings of one's life engage. Sometimes, people who are very vociferous and moralistic are people who have erased the tug of opposition from their lives. They have little sense of the otherness that suffuses and surrounds them. Thus, they can allow themselves all kinds of moral platitudes and even moral judgments of others. It is lonely sometimes to hear them talk because, in their certainty, you can hear the hollow echo of a life only half-lived.

All creativity comes out of that spark of opposition where two different things meet. It is where each one of us was conceived. Masculine and masculine, feminine and feminine on their own cannot procreate. It is the two sides, the two sister oppositions, that create the unity. It is the same rhythm within subjectivity: there is a whole outer side to you, your name, face, role and identity, and there is the hidden world you carry within you. I think that real balance is, in some sense, about action, where the living reality of your life balances what is within you with what you are meeting outside. One of the greatest duties of post-modern culture at the end of this millennium is to try to bring the personal and the communal, the individual and the universal, together.

Experience is working all the time with duality, with that energy of opposition within you. You have no experience that does not have two sides to it. In a certain sense, all of your experience is a kind of narrative or story, with this deep underside that you never see, yet out of which all your possibilities come. Even though it is opaque, it constantly guides you and brings you to places you never expected. That is the surprise and the unpredictability of life. In relation to the notion of balance, we have to begin to strive towards a concept of person or self that is sufficiently complex and substantial to do justice to our huge metaphysical needs at the end of this millennium.

One of the victims of media culture is the depth and interiority of the self. People are treated like images, like instances of general principles, but rarely are individuals taken and illuminated for their own unique depth. The history, narrative and possibilities they carry within themselves are usually sidelined in any description or presentation of them. It is frightening how our collusion with technology has damaged so much our sense of individuality and our sense of the secret and sacred world that every individual inhabits.

Imagination

The imagination is the faculty that gives the duality within us expression and allows its forms of opposition to engage with each other. In the Western Christian tradition we gave a huge role to intellect and to will. The intellect was used to find out what the goal or object was and then the will drove it along the linear track towards it. This model of human sensibility brought us much beauty, but its neglect of the imagination has also cost us dearly. A human life can have everything—beauty, status, reputation, achievement, all kinds of possessions, but if the imagination is not awakened, all these lack presence and depth.

There are poor people who have absolutely nothing, but who have a depth of creative imagination that allows them, even in bleak circumstances, to inhabit a gracious, challenging and exciting world. The heart of it all is that there is an indissoluble, radical, subversive connection between mind and reality. The structures of your mind, the way your mind works, the way your consciousness moves, its patterns, actually determine the world you inhabit. You cannot separate the two of them. The awakened imagination brings us great riches. The imagination is not one-sided; it is passionately interested in wholesomeness and wholeness. The imagination is never tempted or attracted to the flat surface or to whatever is safe and perfect. Sometimes when you hear people talking about the human self you would think that it is made out of stainless steel and is meant to have perfection and purity. But we are clay creatures, striving desperately towards the light.

The idea of the threshold is significant because the human body itself is actually a threshold. Each human individual is a threshold in many different ways. You are a threshold in that you are made out of clay. What keeps you alive is in the invisible air. Yet you belong neither to the earth out of which you have come, nor to the heavens towards which you strain. So, you are always in this oscillation, on this moving threshold. Within your own family you are also on a threshold—the threshold between all of the ancestral lines that meet in you, and the line that will go out from you. In many different ways the imagination tries to awaken, articulate and integrate all the presences that meet in us.

At the beginning of his book *The Phenomenology of Spirit,* Hegel says, *Das wahre ist das ganze,* the truth is whole. Most of the time when we are talking about things, we seem so sure that we are right, yet all we are giving are little minuscule, half-truth glimpses. To become wholesome, we need living connection with the whole. Our access is always limited and partial; yet through the imagination, we can enter more elegantly into its field of creative tensions.

There are two great sentences in the Greek tradition: "Know thyself" and "Everything flows." The human self is surrounded by change and is itself continually changing. Your body is constantly changing. In a philosophy class I once had, our professor told us that over a seven-year period all the cells in our body will have changed. There was at the time someone in England who had been in prison for seven years and he appealed his sentence. His claim was that he was not the person now whom they had sentenced seven years before! So, there is this constant changing. In the West of Ireland, visually we are very aware of this, because the weather and the light change all the time.

If everything was, as the Germans say, in *Stillstand*, or deadlocked in the same position, we would not need to worry about balance. We would all be totally fixated and atrophied in the one position. It is because there is so much movement and change that the notion of balance takes on such depth and urgency. The argument for change is put most memorably by Heraclitus, a philosopher in fifth-century B.C. Greece. He said that you can never step into the same river twice because if you step in at four o'clock and again at five past four, the river has completely changed, and you have changed as well. There is constant change all the time, and imagination is the most faithful force in helping change and continuity maintain a dialogue with each other.

Part of the reason we are so confused at the end of this millennium is that so much change has occurred, at such an acute and relentless pace, that we are not able to decipher and activate the lines of continuity into our own tradition. There is an intense isolation there, a haunting lonesomeness, especially in young people. They are uprooted and dislocated. Even adults a generation or two ahead of them are not able to speak their language. The isolation is intensified in that they are the relentless targets of marketing. Huge multinational marketing systems are targeting teenagers, and what they are achieving is incredible. Parents or teachers could never get teenagers into uniforms and yet multinational corporations have done it. Teenagers are all wearing designer gear. The label is more important than the garment. At the most subversive times of their lives, they are indoctrinated with this peer virus. Again, it is money and greed that have turned teenagers into targets for commodities.

The imagination tries to take change and inhabit it in a way that allows it to be transfigurative rather than destructive. The lovely thing about the imagination is that, whereas the mind often sees change and thinks everything is lost, the imagination can always go deeper than the actual experience of the loss and find something else in it. There is an amazing difference between the way the mind sees something and the way the imagination sees something.

Imagination and the Balance with Otherness

Another lovely quality of the imagination is its passion for otherness. "Otherness" is a technical term, but it means, essentially, everything that is other than you. The easiest way to register the notion of otherness is to think of somebody you dislike intensely. The experience of otherness registers most firmly in what we find strange or totally different from ourselves. One of the huge spiritual, psychological, philosophical and theological problems of post-modern culture is the question of otherness.

The world of media and corporate marketing has actually homogenized things completely and wants to make everything the same. The advertisement you see for Levi's over the Midtown Tunnel as you come into Manhattan is the same as the ad you'll see in Limerick or Dublin or even in the desert or the Middle East. There is an incredible difficulty for individual places and individual experiences to assert their own uniqueness and individuality. It is very difficult in mass culture to argue for a unique space—for what is individual and different. Yet one of the most important conversations in any life remains the conversation with what is other than you. When people get into trouble psychologically, it is often because something comes upon them that frightens them, or paralyzes them, so that they cannot move, work or function. It is something they would never have anticipated in themselves. This sudden confrontation with unexpected otherness becomes crippling. For instance, some people who are perfectionists may find an otherness awakening in or around them that renders them helpless. One of the most threatening forms of otherness in any life is illness. It is a frightening thing that you can be going on with your life, thinking you have troubles, and then you run headlong into serious illness and your life and your world are absolutely altered.

The oppositions that are in us often constellate themselves in other ways, in terms of contradiction. It is interesting to see how the media handles contradiction. The media focuses on an image, but an image is always just one view of a thing, it is never the full view. If you want the full view, you meet with a person face-to-face, or you read good literature or listen to good music or look at a good painting or a good landscape. Then the multidimensionality of a thing comes through. The media is essentially like Plato's Cave—a parade of shadows that we take for the real world. It is a huge subtraction from what is real. To believe in the media as the actual vehicle of truth or the way to "what truly is" can be very misleading. It is necessary to have the kind of exploration that the media does, but on its own as sole authority it is totally insufficient. Its presentations grow ever more syncopated into sound bites.

It is interesting that when the media notices a contradiction in someone, the reportage turns merciless. Usually, it has to do with a fall from a principle, because the media will inevitably have structured the image in the first place in such a way that a certain principle has been embodied. When a contradiction emerges, there is a sensational story. The media "outs" people and, in certain instances where it has a public interest dimension, this can be warranted. More often, however, I believe it is a massive intrusion into the private lives of individuals. While it may make a story today, the media light moves quickly elsewhere, and the exposed individual is left with years of struggle to put his or her life back together again.

What is interesting about contradictions is that each person is a bundle of contradictions. Normally we are not aware of our contradictory nature because there is so much of ourselves that we keep completely hidden. Perhaps one of the reasons we are on this planet is to try to become acquainted with all that is in us. When you meet someone who is not afraid of themselves it is a lovely experience. They might be a mass of contradictions but at least they have patience with their own otherness. I think that, in many ways, the images of self that we see reflected in political life, religious life and media life are totally inadequate to carry the depth that is in us.

In a contradiction, the two sides are meeting. An opposition is happening; it has come alive with great tension and energy. It can be a frightening time in a person's life, but also a very interesting time. Usually, the way we settle and compromise with ourselves is by choosing one side over the other side, and we settle for that reductionism until something awakens the other side, and then the two of them are engaged. I was talking to somebody who was going through a huge conflict trying to decide if he should do A or if he should do B. A wise friend of his said to him, "If it's either/or, it's neither." The idea is that at the heart of the opposition there is something else coming through. That is where I think the notion of balance is really very powerful, because balance is a providential thing that allows something new to emerge from the depths of crisis and contradiction. This suggests faith in a third force that often endeavors to emerge through the oppositions that are coming alive in us.

The Myth of Balance

I want to explore the myth of balance. I am using the word "myth" in two senses. First, in its colloquial sense, the sense that myth is something that is not factually true—it is fantasy. Second, in its more profound sense, which is the idea of the mythical. The great myths are universal stories about dimensions of the gods, of ourselves and of nature. Usually they are stories in which the origin of a thing can be perceived. They are stories of what cannot actually be told. A myth is a narrative. For instance, you have the myth of Genesis, with Adam and Eve in the garden, or the story of Odysseus who got lost and was on his way home for thirty years. Myths and fairy tales are profound communicators of wisdom in very subtle ways. All the folk cultures, even the most ancient ones, always had stories about the way everything began, and these stories in some way were the first attempts to balance people's precarious presence in a strange world. This ties in with the notion of cosmos, which is the idea of order. The *Oxford English Dictionary* includes these two aspects in its definition of "balance." First, balance is "an apparatus for weighing consisting of a beam poised so as to move freely on a central pivot with a scale pan at each end," or second, balance is "the stability due to the equilibrium of forces within a system."

I believe that balance also includes passion, movement, rhythm, urgency and harmony. Balance is not a dead notion. Balance as a monolithic thing would not be balance at all; it would be total imbalance, because there is something in balance that, in order to be what it is, requires the loyal weight of the opposite and opposing force. When you talk about balance, you are talking about the discovery or the unveiling of things, of a secret rhythm of order. I believe that balance can never be merely subjective or monological.

I want to sketch briefly in philosophical terms a cognitive theory of balance. Most theories of balance are non-cognitive and inevitably end up as either strategies or platitudes. There are two main ways of looking at balance—the conservative and liberal views, or the empiricist and the idealist views. The first one is that balance is a strategy. You hear people saying that you must have balance in your life. If you do not have balance, everything will turn chaotic. Balance, then, is an external frame imposed on experience from the outside. It controls things and keeps the chaos away.

Such strategies of balance are often no more than veiled repression. For instance, you may feel a deep complexity of feeling, but you pretend that you do not feel. You bury everything in the basement of your mind. Jung used to call this "the return of the repressed." No sooner have you expelled something that you cannot accept about yourself out the front door than it has made its way in the back door and is waiting there to confront you again. It is a strange thing about consciousness that if you try deliberately to get rid of something or to stop thinking about something, you only end up reinforcing it.

This idea finds humorous expression in a story I heard

somewhere. A man went to see a guru as he was finding it difficult to meditate because his mind was scattered. The guru said to him, "I want you to go home and not think about monkeys." Surprised at the advice, because monkeys never figured in his mind, the man nevertheless returned home intending to carry out the advice. Once at home, he started to try not to think about monkeys. First there was one monkey and then there were two monkeys, then there were ten monkeys. Within two hours he was back to the guru as his mind had become an exclusive monkey jungle. Thus, there is a strange thing in consciousness, in the mind, that if you make an issue of something it can expand and possess you. This seems to be what happens with bitterness. A bitter person cannot decide to be bitter between 7:00 and 7:30 on Saturday evenings, because if you are bitter, it is within you everywhere. Resentment is exactly the same kind of thing. Resentment, bitterness, defeat, despair, even depression—all of these share this pervasive quality. When I sit in front of somebody who is clinically, chronically depressed, the feeling that I have sometimes is that the person is not actually there. The fascinating question is, where are they? So repression is often the outcome when balance is approached as a functional, imposed strategy.

Another dimension of balance as a functional strategy is fear. If you are afraid of things, you will stay in line; this often has to do with authority. On German television, in the last six or seven weeks, on the tenth anniversary of the fall of East Germany, they have been replaying old news excerpts. It is unbelievable viewing. Two days before the whole thing started, there was Honecker, leader of East Germany, with all the leaders of the Communist world, and they were all paying tribute to one another. Ceausescu was in the middle of them. And the whole facade was within inches of collapsing, never to return. Flexibility is balance and balance is flexibility. When a thing hardens it cannot bend. It can only break. When a thing or system becomes totally atrophied, the smallest incision can cause the whole thing to vanish as if it were a false garment.

Another dimension of balance as a functional strategy, one that also keeps people in line, is the whole world of religious edict and theology. Many people in Ireland held their lives in a certain kind of balance because they were theologically terrified. We are coming out of that now. This theory of balance, which is a frame from outside, usually works with an unexamined belief in the given facts. It is very empiricist, it is one-dimensional, and it is usually ideological. It is non-cognitive in the sense that it is never worked out nor its deeper grounding ever questioned. It is given, and because it is given, it is always in the service of some elite group or some vested interest that wants the balance to hold for some ideological reason.

The opposite view of balance is that balance is a purely subjective invention—I can invent, sustain and implement my own order. This, of course, is equally false. Literary tragedy, for instance, unmasks this as illusion. Tragedy presents great passionate individuals who attempt to establish their own order and their action brings them into total conflict with the hidden order, which uncoils on top of them and completely changes the world they inhabit. Therefore, balance is neither a fixed empirical thing nor an invented, subjective thing. Rather, balance is an implicit equilibrium that emerges in the fair play of opposing forces—opposing sister forces.

Balance yields itself in the dialogue and dialectic of passionate forces. It is not monological. Much of what passes for conversation in post-modern culture is merely intercepting monologues. If you watch television programs or listen to the radio, you hear little true conversation. When you yourself are involved in a really genuine conversation with another person, you will remember it for weeks because something unexpected shifts or happens in the dynamic of conversation. It is no accident that at the infancy of Western culture we have the great models of conversation in Plato's dialogues. In true dialogue something truly other and unexpected emerges. What I am talking about here is a theory of growth; not economic growth, but the growth of life and experience that works in this shifting balance between dialogue on the one hand and dialectic on the other hand.

It is interesting to consider balance in terms of the

physical human body, in terms of anatomy. The French phenomenologist Merleau-Ponty has wonderful things to say about the human body. The body is not an object to think about. Rather, it is a grouping of lived-through meanings, which move towards equilibrium. Your body is not just an object, it is actually all the meanings that people have towards your body. It is moving towards equilibrium. The place where your balance is regulated is also the place where your hearing and listening are activated. This is in the fluid of the semicircular canals of the inner ear. The eighth nerve goes through this liquid in the inner ear. It gives the impulses to the brain and tells the brain where you are. For instance, in cases of vertigo, where there is irritation or some damage, you have the feeling that the room has actually moved, but of course it has not. People also have that experience "the morning after the night before," when you suddenly think that the laws of causality have changed and that the room is shifting around.

Therefore, true balance in the body is linked to listening, but also metaphorically, true balance is linked to an attentiveness that allows you to engage fully with a situation, a person or your culture or memory so that the hidden balance within can emerge. Listening can actually be a force that elicits the balance and allows it to emerge. Balance is not subjective. Neither is balance to be simply achieved or reached by human beings. True balance is a grace. It is something that is given to you. When you watch somebody walking the high wire, you know that they could tumble any second. That is the way we all are. Though we prefer to forget and repress it, we live every moment in the condition of contingency. There are people who got up this morning, prepared for another normal day, but something happened, some event, news, disappointment or something wonderful, and their lives will never be the same after this day in the world. This is a day they will never forget. Very often our actual balance in the world as we go is totally precarious, without our realizing it. Balance invites us not to take ourselves too seriously.

I spent five years in Germany and I loved German culture, music, thinking and philosophy. But the Germans would not be known as post-graduates in the whole area of humor or spontaneity! There is in the Irish psyche, I think, a kind of flexibility and a grounding humor that actually levels things and balances things out. I have talked to people who worked with Irish people in all kinds of areas in the Third World where there was poverty and war. They often said that the Irish brought a certain humor into the situation that allowed others to forget for a while the awfulness that was around them. This, of course, is a direct derivative of our history. We have had a history of incredible pain, misery, poverty and suffering in this country, which is often forgotten now. In these politically correct and tiger economic times, it is embarrassing to remember what has happened to us. The truth is that terrible things happened to us. And the only way we were able to come through it was to win some distance from it. Often, Irish humor has this subtext of knowing the complete horror, but yet deciding not to bend to its ravages. That is why Beckett is a sublime Irish writer, because he can bring the bleakness and the humor to such incredible balance and harmony.

Balance can be beautifully achieved in the human body, especially in dance. I remember, one night in Lisdoonvarna, watching, in a small little corner of the pub, about thirty-five human bodies starting to dance. There was a band playing and I saw these people and I thought to myself that they could never dance in such a small space. Yet, when the music started and brought rhythm, they were wheeling in and out and nobody crashed into anyone else. So sometimes when another rhythm is present, balance becomes possible in the most unpredictable situations.

Balance and the Millennium

In the concluding section, I want to reflect on balance at the millennium threshold. A millennium threshold is said to be a time of imbalance and disturbance. To be honest, I believe that much of the excitement about the millennium is a result of manipulation. For a few cultures, this is not the millennium. If you could talk to stones and rivers and oceans or even sheep, they would be asking why these humans are getting worked up about the millennium. The earth and the ocean and the rain and the wind and the trees and the cows and the calves have no idea that we are entering a new millennium. But, because we are all fixated on the millennium, there is a lot happening and it is a huge threshold; and in a way we are coming into it vulnerable and very exposed.

There are several agents of imbalance. One is the whole consumerist trend of post-modern culture. In philosophical terms what is going on here is a reduction of the "who" question about presence and person, to the "what" question and the "how" question. It's an obsession, almost a regression to what Freud called the "oral stage." The key tenet here is that consumption creates identity. I was over in Atlanta, Georgia, on a book tour early on in the year. I saw a weed there called kudzu; it grows a foot in a day. This weed is set to take over, and if it's not cut back it will take over completely. It struck me as a profound image for consumerism. Most of us are moving through such an undergrowth of excess that we cannot sense the shape of ourselves anymore. Sometimes you meet a writer who gives you a little instrumentation to make a clearance here. For me, such a writer is William Stafford, the wonderful American poet. In the latest book from his estate on the nature of poetry, *Crossing Unmarked Snow,* here are four sentences:

The things you do not have to say make you rich.
Saying the things you do not have to say
  weakens your talk.
Hearing the things you do not need to hear
  dulls your hearing.
The things you know before you hear them,
  those are you and
this is reason that you are in the world.

There is a massive functionalism at the heart of our times, a huge imbalance in post-modernity, primarily because certain key conversations are not taking place. One conversation that is not taking place is a conversation between the privileged and the poor. We are an immensely privileged minority. We think the Western world is the whole world. Yet, in fact, we are just a tiny minority. The majority of the world is living in the most awful circumstances. A friend of mind in London who has done research on this told me that 80 percent of the people in the world have never used a telephone. It is a sobering statistic. What disturbs me morally is the fact that we are here now in a comfortable setting talking about things we love. At the moment, there is a woman, a young mother, going through a dustbin in some barrio in South America for the tenth time today, for crumbs for her starving children whom she loves just as much as we love our children. The disturbing question is why is that person out there carrying that and why can we be here in comfort? I do not know the answer, but I do know that we are privileged and that the duty of privilege is absolute integrity. That is a huge part of balance, the question of integrity and integration. Without integrity, there can be no true integration.

Another conversation that is not happening, which is a terrifying non-event, is the conversation between the Western culture and Islam. Certain people are making attempts to do it, such as Edward Said, the cultural and literary critic, the NPR reporter Jacki Lyden, the theologian Michael Sells. Yet it is a conversation that is not happening essentially at a cultural level. We have a caricature of what Islam is. They have the same caricature of us. In caricature and false imagery and projection, so much violence, destruction and wars are already seeded. It is bleakly ironic in a culture that is obsessed with communication technology that the actual art and vital content of communication is shrinking all the time. In relation to the Irish context, there is an urgent need for greater dialogue between the forces of city culture and the rural domain. The city has become the power center in Western culture. It is where the most significant powers of media, finance, politics and religion are located. Naturally, then, the media, in reflecting these activities, inevitably does so through an urban filter of language, thought and style. Were one to watch the television every night for a week to see what images from rural life emerge on television, one would find few real references to the life on the land. Also the public language describing rural life is a language determined by the city and it is usually not an understanding language. People who live in the country know that you have to live in the country to know what the country is actually like. The country is not so much a community, it is a network. It has deep, intricate thickets of connection that cannot be seen from outside. Folk-life has depth and shadow that the media never comes near. The language used by the media about the country often reveals its distance from the cut and thrust of the rural sensibility. Even the word "rural" is diminutive. If one looks around for words about farming, to show the beauty and profound dignity of what it is, it is difficult to find any words in the public forum. I think farming is one of the great life callings. It has become very difficult now, but it is a great artistic, creative calling.

To Find Balance in an Ireland
of Inner Turbulence

At the threshold of the millennium, Ireland is in some turbulence. Many of the sacred facades have been pulled down in the domains of religion, politics and finance. The unmasking has revealed corruption in all of these domains. These revelations have dulled and damaged our sense of and belief in ideals. They have caused disillusionment and cynicism. The positive side of this is that it relieves us of over-dependence on false crutches; it invites us to depend more on our own courage and critique. But, there is a danger in all of this clearing out that we will throw out many of the values that have sustained, refined and deepened us as a people. I do believe that Ireland has something very special, something very unique in Europe, and we really are at a crossroads with it. Of course, not everything was perfect. With the old kind of lifestyle, there was a lot of poverty, drudgery and slavery of work. There were the valleys of the squinting windows. There was the awful repression of the 1930s and 1940s in Ireland, when so many lovely innocent people were totally sinned against in the most sinister ways. There is that negative shadow in our tradition. But this is not the full story. Our tradition also has huge spiritual, imaginative and wisdom riches. There was a sense of proportion, a sense of belonging, a sense of being in a tradition that we are now in danger of losing completely.

Ireland is predominantly a folk culture. The issue for me at the level of principle is that it seems to take hundreds of years for a folk culture to weave itself, and yet so often, with the infusion of the consumerism virus, such a cultural fabric unravels in a very short time. The question then is: what hidden resources are there within our culture that can help us to stand at this very severing crossroads and still hold what is precious to us from our tradition, to guide us over the threshold into the new millennium? It is a very important question because many people who are spiritually, theologically and philosophically awakened look to Ireland and see something here that we ourselves often do not see. It will demand a great vision and leadership to engage all the tensions of our present turbulence and find a path that still vitally connects with the heart of the Irish tradition and yet engages the modern milieu openly and creatively. A tradition is a living presence. To reacquaint ourselves with the brightness as well as the darkness in our tradition could be an important first step.

The pace and rate of development in contemporary Ireland is quite alarming. Ireland seems to be a huge target for major development. There are people who would sell everything for any kind of development and short-term gain. This is difficult to comprehend, given the terrible history we have had of being exiled from our own land. Now that we have finally got the land, it is almost as if we are not able to be at ease with it and inhabit it and recognize its beauty. I am not saying that there should be no development—of course there should be. People need to live. I am saying that we should have greater openness towards forms of development that do not destroy our environment. It is hugely important because it is not just ours—we are custodians of it for our children, who will inhabit it after us.

A government is elected constitutionally to protect a people against conquest, yet the economic consumerist conquest that is going on in Ireland is just unbelievable. In Connemara, the people say, *Tá an nádúr ag imeacht as na daoine,* the nature is going out of people. When people have very little, it is natural for them to be close. I am not romanticizing poverty; it is a horrible thing, full of drudgery. Think of all the people who had to emigrate because there was nothing for them. But yet there was some kind of *nádúr,* or closeness. It seems to be impossible for a culture to develop economically and get really rich and yet maintain the same *nádúr* and closeness. So the question is: where could we find new places to awaken something in us in order that we do not lose that sense of *nádúr* and of belonging with each other?

Our heritage, rather than being something that can enable us to stand critically, worthily and courageously on the threshold of this new millennium, is now being converted into almost a fast-food product, that can be read off in ten minutes by a visiting tour bus somewhere. This is a very important issue. There is an ancient memory and a tradition that has huge archaic layers. We should be a lot more confident and a lot more courageous as we go into the new millennium, and we should try to work with an idea of balance that is equal to that complex history and that somehow allows us to stand with a critical sense at the edge of this new millennium and cross over with a certain kind of confidence.

For Equilibrium

Like the joy of the sea coming home to shore,
May the relief of laughter rinse through your
    soul.

As the wind loves to call things to dance,
May your gravity be lightened by grace.

Like the dignity of moonlight restoring the
    earth,
May your thoughts incline with reverence and
    respect.

As water takes whatever shape it is in,
So free may you be about who you become.

As silence smiles on the other side of what's said,
May your sense of irony bring perspective.

As time remains free of all that it frames,
May your mind stay clear of all it names.

May your prayer of listening deepen enough
To hear in the depths the laughter of God.

From *To Bless the Space Between Us*

AGING

"Old age can be a time of great
liberation and freedom."

The six-part series "L Plus" was a prac-
tical guide to the later years of life.
One aspect of those years that needed to be
addressed was the onset of old age and ultimately mortality. John had written so posi-
tively and poetically in *Anam Cara* about
aging and death that I wished to include
him as a contributor to the series. This conversation was recorded in the office of Mar-
riage Relationship and Counseling Services
in Dublin, where John had given a talk in
April 1998.

THE NEGATIVE SIDE

One of the amazing recognitions of Celtic spirituality and wisdom is the sisterhood of nature and the soul. The body is made out of clay. It has the memory of the earth in it, and not just the memory of the earth, but also in some strange, subtle, almost silent way, it has the rhythms of the seasons in it too. G. B. Shaw said that youth is wasted on the young, so springtime is always a season that somehow resembles the energy of youth. Autumntime seems to mirror the gathering and the harvest of old age. One of the amazing lines in the Bible that I really like is a line from the prophet Haggai, who says, "You have sown so much and harvested so little." I feel that old age and aging is a time of great gathering, a time of sifting and a time of reaping the rewards of forgotten and neglected experience. Contemporary society worships youth: it worships strength; it worships image. It has a whole ideology of externality and it has no refined sense of the subtlety of the soul, the secrecy of the heart. Especially, it has no sensitivity of these interim regions where the great gatherings happen in human life.

Admittedly old age is a very difficult time—and I can't talk about it from within because I still have a bit of youth left in me!—but it is a time when the body becomes more infirm, when you could be ill, when you could be alone, and it is also a time maybe when you become dependent. When I think of my own future and getting old, one of the things that would really disturb me would be my lack of autonomy and freedom, that I could be dependent on other people to go places, to take me out, to mind me, to get things for me, bring things in to me. I think that we need in our society to be very sensitive to that diminishing of the body's vigor and passion and possibility and the lack of freedom that goes with that, especially when illness comes in old age. It must be very frightening for a person if you're trying to forget that death is ahead and you're trying to live every day as it comes, yet illness comes. Illness is the precursor of death when you're old, and it frightens you, and small illness knocks a lot more out of you than it would have when you were a young person. So there is that whole tide of negativity that the old have to deal with. When you walk down the street and see an old person walking slowly, you just overtake them and go on. But you wouldn't notice the achievement of that person looking for what they need, shopping or whatever, and being able to come back home. When an old person goes for a day out and comes back home and recovers from it, it's almost a celebration.

It reminds me of the great Polish director Kieślowski, who made *The Ten Commandments* and *Three Colors*. Always in his films there is a crucial moment in the evolution of the plot when an old man or an old woman, anonymous figures, just pass by and the camera lingers on them. It is like an oracle or an omen of the future of time for these characters, who are in the midst of great passion and trying to work things out.

HARVEST TIME

So there is a negative side to old age, but that has to do with the externality. It has to do with the body, and my understanding of old age and aging is that as the body diminishes, the soul gets richer. In old age, one of the things you have, whatever way you want to construct it, is time. When you have time, your soul begins to decipher things more and more. Camus said that after one day in the world, we could live the rest of our life in solitary confinement, because so much happens to us in one day. If you look at that from the perspective of all of one's life, there are thousands of years of experience packed into sixty or seventy years of human life, because the amazing thing about the human mind is it is never neutral. The amazing thing about the human soul and the human spirit is it is never in a state of non-experience. There is something going on all the time. Even when you are sleeping. There are rivers of dream-thought flowing through the earth of your body, bringing up all types of mythic, archetypal stuff, some of which belongs to you, a lot of which belongs to the clay and a lot of which belongs to the race. A human being is an endless, epic theater of activity. So in old age, time slows a bit, the outer draw to activity recedes, and you have time for the more contemplative side of things. One enters the contemplative side of one's own life, and you have a chance then to decipher what has happened to you, to see the hidden depths of experiences that have occurred in your life. You really have a chance to weave a new shelter for yourself. I love the image of the Carthusian monks, the contemplatives, who wear this habit with a cowl on it, and that then is sewn up when they die and becomes the shroud in which they are laid out. I would look at old age in a positive way, as a time of weaving the eternal shroud, the things that you take with you into the eternal world.

I remember one time in Moycullen giving a sermon about how we shouldn't get waylaid; our journeys shouldn't get falsified, trying to carry the world on our shoulders, because we can take nothing with us when we die. I was up in the local shop afterwards, and one of the neighbors said to me that he liked the sermon and he said, "Do you know the way we say that around here? You'd never see a trailer after a hearse!" You can take nothing with you but the interior things, which have reached a level of refinement that there is no barrier that they have to pass through. In that sense, aging is the ultimate refinement and ultimate harvest.

Our culture has gone so much into falsity that we don't acknowledge that at all. It is very interesting, if you look at the anthropology of tribal cultures, that the elders were always the people of wisdom. Nowadays, we put them away in old people's homes. Sometimes people have to be put into old people's homes when they can't be managed, but some of the loneliest places I've ever been are old people's homes. I remember one particular place I used to visit. When you went in, twenty little worn, winnowed faces with hungry eyes would look up at you as if you might be the visitor that they've expected maybe for months, or maybe in some cases for years. It used to take me a couple of days to recover from it, because it is so lonesome. It's lovely to have a friendship with an old person, because you learn so much from them. The Bible says that you should always ask for advice from a wise person. Old age and wisdom usually go together, because when you've been through the treadmill of experience you know what counts. You know the chaff from the real grain that brings nourishment. Old people have great wisdom and great light, and when they are not governed by fear there is incredible permission in them. You often get more encouragement in relation to your own wildness and sense of danger and carelessness from an old person than from anyone who is stuck in the middle of a system or a role or the kind of atrophied complacency that often passes for achievement and respectability.

THE GIFT OF MEMORY

Since I was a child, one of the things that always haunted me was the way everything passes away. In relation to death, that is the ultimate transience, when someone you love goes away, falls away out of visibility into the invisibility of death. I often think there is a place where our vanished days gather, and that place is memory. One of the fascinating things about old people is the way that they stay around the well of memory. If you are willing to sit with them, you won't get analytical sentences from them about was it this or was it that, or could the meaning have been one, two, three. What you will always get is narrative about events from their childhood, which are never straight replications of what happened, but are the bones of the event, enfleshed with image and with anecdote and with narrative. In a strange way, nothing is ever lost or forgotten; everything that befalls us remains within us. There is within you the presence in a refined sense of everything that has ever happened to you, and if you go looking for it you will find it. I always think that in our time, memory has been hijacked by the computer industry, and the more correct term is "recall" rather than "memory." Memory is a particularly intimate and sacramental human phenomenon and there is a great depth and density to everyone. The image in nature that is really profound in relation to that is the tree; all the rings of memory enfold all the years of growing, blossoming, dying, budding, blossoming, growing, dying, and enfold all the elements of experience. In a similar way, within the clay part of each soul, the rings of memory are there and you can find them.

A lot of the experiences that we have in the world are torn, broken, hard experiences, and in broken, difficult, lonesome experiences you earn a quality of light that is very precious. I often think of it as quarried light. When you come through a phase of pain or isolation or suffering, the light that is given to you at the end of that is a very precious light, and really when you go into something similar again, it is the only kind of light that can mind you. It is the lantern that will bring you through that pain.

One of our difficulties in contemporary culture is this massive amnesia. We forget so much because we are addicted to the moment. If sad, difficult things have happened to you, and you have earned quarried light, again and again you should visit the light, and almost like the light around the tabernacle that signals the presence, you should allow that light to come round you to awaken the presence that is in you, to calm you, to bring you contentment, and as well to bring you courage. When a person is aging, one of the things he really needs is courage.

I love the word "careless." You know the way people say, "Well, he's a careless kind of an individual." In one sense, that can mean that there is no responsibility in him. In its literal sense it can mean that he is care-less, that there are no false burdens of care on him, and that when he comes to the threshold of an experience, he enters it with full availability, full courage and full wildness. It would be lovely in old age, as the body sheds its power, if each of us who would be pilgrims into that time could shed the false gravity and the weight that we carry for a lot of our lives and if we could enter our old age almost like a baby enters childhood, with the same kind of gracefulness, of possibility, and the same kind of innocence, but a second innocence rather than a first one.

POSSIBILITY

There is great wisdom in the mystical tradition and in the Catholic tradition, and the Catholic tradition always recognized that the contemplatives need ritual to make their way through the deserts of solitude. If you sit down in an armchair by the fire and you allow the days, like big empty gray rooms, to come around your head, you will turn and feed on your own negativity. Contemplatives survive because the day is divided into times of praise, prayer, ritual, and in order to survive solitude one needs ritual. There is really no kind of education for getting old. You get old, you begin to lose your power, suddenly you find that you are left with it, you are on your own with it, and no one sees it like you do. There is so much that could be done to make people aware of the possibilities that are in old age. Old age, like illness, is a time when you really need to mind yourself. If you get hooked on some of the down-pulls of gravity in your soul, it can be a time of torture so that you pray for release—to die would be total peace. If you look on it as a time of possibility, amazing things can happen. A good axiom in life is to try to see the possibilities in a situation. Often in a situation, it is the walls we see, it is the door where the key has been thrown away that we see, and we never see the windows of possibilities and the places where thoughts and feelings can grow. In old age there is a lot more time, and freedom comes with that. In old age one can totally reorient one's life and find fascinating companionship with one's own soul.

How we view the future actually shapes that future. Time isn't like space at all. When you think of space, you think of Connemara with the mountains stretching out with no walls at all, and if you look at Clare you see the little fields and the space stretching out towards the mountains and towards the ocean. We falsely think that time is like that too. You walk through the field of today and then you cross over to the field of tomorrow and then to the field of the day after that. But it's not like that. Time comes towards us unshapen, predominantly, and it is our expectation that shapes the time that is coming. So expectation creates the future. If you bring creative expectation to your future, no matter what difficulty may lie in wait for you, you will be able somehow to transfigure it. Whereas if you bring really negative expectation to your future, you will turn yourself totally into a tower of misery. It is amazing actually, when people are in limit threshold situations, the resources they can call on which they would have never been aware of until it really gets very difficult. *Nuair a thagann an crú ar an tairne,* as they say in Connemara—when the pressure comes on you. There's great wisdom in perspective and distance. It is usually when we are myopic and close up to a thing and we can't see its contour at all, that it totally imprisons and controls us. Whereas sometimes when you step back, you get another view, and you pick up a way of relating to the event or the situation which frees you predominantly.

One of the most beautiful films I have ever seen is a film by the Japanese director Kurosawa. It's called *Dersu Uzala,* and it is told about a platoon of Russian soldiers who go in to map an area of Outer Mongolia. The leader of the troop is a very elegant, dignified, intellectual man, and he comes across an old Mongolian man who is very wise. An amazing friendship builds between the two men, which is a classical theme in literature—the mentor and the disciple—and they get very close. The young man is learning so much from the older man and they deepen this amazing spiritual friendship, but what the young man doesn't realize is that his passion, his sense of life, his curiosity are enabling the old man to prepare for his dying. There is one famous moment in the film when the old man suddenly sees a tiger, and it is a moment of pure dark epiphany. You know in that moment that he knows he is going to die, and the rest of the film just fills out the moment. It is an amazing film about a way of ritual-izing one's leave-taking of the world—with dignity, with courage, with great peacefulness, and as well with a sense of what you are actually leaving behind to those that you love.

TEMPERAMENT, NOT TIME

There is a story that my brother told me about a pub near us at home. You would never get a lift going to the pub if you wanted to get there. You would go to a little village in order to get back. He was driving home one evening and he was passing this man who was going in the direction he was driving in, so he said, "Will you sit in, John?" and John said, "No. Even though I'm walking this way, I'm going the other way!" It is a good metaphor for the false direction that masquerades as power and as achievement in contemporary culture. A lot of that is misdirected, and we need to steady ourselves and have a look at where we actually are. I really believe that age depends on temperament, rather than on time. I know people who at twenty-six and twenty-seven with the gravity that is around them, the seriousness, the lack of any little bit of spring or wildness in them are really about ninety! I know people of seventy, eighty and even eighty-five years who have the minds of seventeen-year-olds! They never managed to get old at all! For some strange reason, the passionate heart never ages, and if you keep your eros and your passion alive, then in some subtle, inevitable way, you are already in the eternal world. Several years ago I wrote a poem called "Cottage." It is about time and the fact that we don't recognize the days that we have; and part of the lack of integration in our lives is that we feel they don't recognize us either—

Cottage

I sit, alert
behind the small window
of my mind and watch
the days pass,
strangers,
who have no reason
to look in.

From *Echoes of Memory*

LONELINESS

I think that it is impossible for a human to be lonely. I know that sounds absolutely crazy, but the example I would give is when I left Connemara and lived in Germany for four and a half years. I was a bit shocked at first because I knew Connemara very well and I was very close to the humans there, and suddenly when I was in Germany in an apartment on my own, it was utterly solitary. If you want to get away from humans, and you want to be really on your own, Germany is a great place to go! The people don't bother you at all—if they want to come and visit you they will ring you up beforehand. What struck me was the dual nature of the mind, the inner companionship of yourself. When you say "Hello" to someone, you are breaking in to a conversation they are always having with themselves. So we are always actually in permanent dialogue with ourselves, and therefore solitude is a very rich time. It is the purification of that dialogue. I think what happens in loneliness is that we panic; we somehow see ourselves as isolated and distant from others, and then we really feel abandoned. And there are a lot of people very lonely because they are literally abandoned. Nobody cares about them. There are a lot of other people in relationships, in connection, who are cared for and loved, and they still feel lonely. That is their own responsibility. They feel self-pity, or they feel obsessed with themselves, whereas if they let the rhythm of their solitude run and trusted it, they would be grand. I have learned myself painfully that you can only relate to someone if you somehow have the courage and the need to inhabit your own solitude. You can only relate out of your separateness, otherwise you are just using the other person to shield you from your own solitude. Old age puts you right into confrontation with that possibility, opens it up to you and calls on you to trust and to honor the eternal thing that maybe has been sleeping within you.

LIBERATION

Old age is a time of great freedom. One of the things that militates against freedom for most humans is the weight of responsibility—all they have to do, and their constant obsession with the current project and with the project of life. If there are people depending on you, you have made your responsibilities and you are on the go all the time. You have a whole barrage of expectations coming towards you. You are part of a system or a network which is coming towards you as well, and you have so little space and so little free time for who you really are, for what you would really love to do, for what really deeply concerns you. That is why an awful lot of people in contemporary culture postpone their real lives until they retire.

They work like hell to get everything worked out and everything achieved, and then they believe that when they have that done, they will have time to enjoy. Some of them do actually achieve it. But sometimes if you get into that habit too deeply, you become what you do, and even when you have the time, you are not actually able to enjoy it. Ideally, old age can be a time of great liberation and freedom. It is a time when a lot of the social mystification and mythology calms down, and you return to the essence of things. I think it is not accidental that the body is pared down in old age, because it is part of the creative process. If you are writing a poem, you might have fifty versions of the poem, and might ultimately end up with six or seven lines after maybe having written sixteen hundred lines. The distilled essence comes out. I think in old age, with the paring down of the body, the paring down of social connection and the paring down of mobility, there is a chance for the distilled essence to actually show itself. You often glimpse that distillation in the faces or the eyes of old people. To put it another way, old age is a time of theater. Very often the old body is the ultimate actor's disguise, and inside that old body is pure distilled essence, and it is a gracious, sacramental moment when you meet it. Patrick Kavanagh has said that we were taught to prepare for life rather than to live it.

That is maybe the primary intention of all holiness, spirituality and love—to free us for our lives. Gabriel García Márquez said somewhere that to live is an art, and no sooner have we begun to learn it than it is already time for us to be departing. There are people now at this moment confronted with their leave-taking. They will be going out of the world in an hour, in a week or whatever, and would give anything to have another week or a month or a year, and they won't have it. And here are we, even if we are old, we still have time, and time is always full of possibility. It would really be a great gift that an old person could give to themselves, the gift of recognizing the possibilities that are in that time, and to use their imagination. The imagination is the gateway to a full life, and people who awaken their imagination come in to a force field of possibility and there are doors opening everywhere. I think it is unknown what you can do if you begin to see it. But so often, we allow the image that other people have of us to stop us from entering our lives and we become literally what they want. I think in old age you are gone beyond that! You have wild permission! Old people could become very subversive and very fascinating if they actually claimed the possibilities that they had and if they talked out a bit more, said what they feel and didn't stand back and let the so-called young people, the yuppies and the entrepreneurs, run the whole show. Old people have far more fascinating things to say than an awful lot of what passes for wisdom in contemporary culture. It would be lovely to hear them speak.

One of the most amazing poets of the twentieth century is Czesław Miłosz, and he has a beautiful poem on old age called "A New Province." There is a lovely line from another poet, Derek Walcott, where he says, "Feast on your life." There is nothing more beautiful that can be put on the table of your mind than the feast of your own life. To put it another way altogether and to use a Catholic metaphor: every person's life is a Eucharist, an individual Eucharist, and you are the priestess or the priest who makes the sacrament of your own life happen, and so we should get dangerously into celebrating.

There is also a poem from Octavio Paz that I love. It is one of the poems in his amazing collection *Eagle or Sun?* and it is about old age as a time of liberation from all the falsities that you burdened yourself with:

> With great difficulty, advancing by millimeters
>   each year,
> I carve a road out of the rock.
> For millennia my teeth have wasted and my
>   nails broken
> to get there, to the other side,
> to the light and the open air.
> And now that my hands bleed and my teeth
>   tremble,
> unsure, in a cavity cracked by thirst and dust,
> I pause and contemplate my work:
> I have spent the second part of my life
> breaking the stones, drilling the walls, smashing
>   the doors,
> removing the obstacles I placed between the
>   light and myself
> in the first part of my life.

For Old Age

May the light of your soul mind you.

May all your worry and anxiousness about your age
Be transfigured.

May you be given wisdom for the eyes of your soul
To see this as a time of gracious harvesting.
May you have the passion to heal what has hurt you,
And allow it to come closer and become one
      with you.

May you have great dignity,
And a sense of how free you are,
Above all, may you be given the wonderful gift
Of meeting the eternal light that is within you.

May you be blessed;
And may you find a wonderful love
In your self for your self.

From *To Bless the Space Between Us*

DEATH

"Death . . . is a time of great homecoming,
and there is no need to be afraid."

The same location as for the conversation on aging—a city center office in Dublin. Death follows naturally from old age. For John, it was not to be feared. It would be "a very beautiful meeting between you and yourself" and there would be "a great fiesta time ahead."

COMING HOME

Death is the unseen companion, the unknown companion who walks every step of the journey with us. It came out of the womb with us and has been with us till now and is here with us today. Part of the art of living, creative living, is to transfigure the different difficulties that you have, the negative things in your life. As you begin to transfigure them, what you are ultimately transfiguring is the presence of your own death. And then when death comes to you at the end, it won't be a monster expelling you against your will from the shelter of your familiarity. In many ways, death could become the truest image of your own life and your own self. Maybe at death, there is a very beautiful meeting between you and yourself, and then you go together into the invisible kingdom where there is no more darkness, suffering, separation or sadness, and where you are one with all those that you love in the seen world and in the unseen world. Death in that sense is a time of great homecoming, and there is no need to be afraid.

If you could interview a baby in the womb, a baby that was about to be born, and the baby asked you what is going to happen to it and you said, "You are going to go through a very dark channel. You are going to be pushed out. You are going to arrive into a vacant world of open air and light. The cord that connects you to your mother is going to be cut. You are going to be on your own forevermore, and regardless of how close you come to another, you will never belong in the way you have been able to belong here." The baby would have no choice but to conclude that it was going to die! Maybe death is that way too. As it seems that we die from inside the womb of the world, we are born into a new world where space and time and all the separation and all the difficulties no longer assail us. We are coming home! My father, Lord have mercy on him, used always say, "Eye hath not seen, nor ear heard, what the Lord has prepared for those who love him." So there is a great fiesta time ahead, and we would want to be practicing if we haven't been any good at it in this world. We would want to be practicing, even against our will, a certain little bit of happiness, because we could be really deluged with pleasure in the next life.

THE ETERNAL WORLD

Death is actually a rebirth. At our first birth, we came out of the darkness of the unknown. Then came our life here, before we return at death into the unknown. Samuel Beckett captured this wonderfully in a very short little play, *Breath*. It begins with a birth cry. Breathing follows and then the death-sigh. The soul is freed into a world where there is no more darkness and indeed no more space and time as we knew it in this world. So where does the soul go? Meister Eckhart had a simple answer to that. It goes nowhere. The eternal world is not some faraway galaxy that we haven't discovered yet. The eternal world is here. The dead are here with us, invisible to us, but we can sense their presence. They are looking out for us.

For us time is linear, but for the dead it is more a circle of eternity. John Moriarty, the wonderful Kerry philosopher, says that time is eternity living dangerously. That is his magic sentence and it is so true. The Celtic people did not divide time from eternity. They were *fite fuaite,* woven into each other. Eternity is not an extension of time, but it is pure presence, pure belonging. When you are in the eternal, you are outside of nothing. You are within every-thing, enjoying the fullest participation. There is no more separation. It is what the contemplative medieval scholars called the Beatific Vision, where the eye with which you see God is God's eye seeing you. You are embraced in the purest circle of love. You are everywhere and you are no-where, but you are in complete presence.

THE END OR THE BEGINNING?

Death is going to come. No one has been able to stop it yet! The Connemara people say, *Ní féidir dul i bhfolach ar an mbás*—you cannot hide from death. We fear it because we do not know how, when or where it will come, but come it will. Yet we still have great freedom about the way we approach it. We should not think negatively or destructively about it, but rather see the possibilities that are in it. Of course there is a lonesomeness in it. Of course there is fright in it, going into the unknown, but we have been given wonderful shelters about the belonging that is in it. It is not a dark end but the beginning of a path of new brightness. If we can learn not to fear death, we have literally nothing to fear.

Entering Death

I pray that you will have the blessing
Of being consoled and sure about your death.

May you know in your soul
There is no need to be afraid.

When your time comes, may you have
Every blessing and strength you need.

May there be a beautiful welcome for you
In the home you are going to.

You are not going somewhere strange,
Merely back to the home you have never left.

May you live with compassion
And transfigure everything
Negative within and about you.

When you come to die,
May it be after a long life.
May you be tranquil
Among those who care for you.

May your going be sheltered
And your welcome assured.
May your soul smile
In the embrace
Of your Anam Cara.

From *To Bless the Space Between Us*

POSTSCRIPT

In a revealing interview published in Dublin's *Sunday Tribune* on Christmas Day 2005, John spoke with Suzanne Power about death.

ONE OF THE LONELIEST PLACES IN THE WORLD to be is at a deathbed where the one who is departing is haunted by regret for their unlived life. One of the greatest sins is the unlived life. If my own death were to occur tomorrow, what would be the peaks of my existence? The faces of my beloved, and of others I love and those who love me. The dark valleys of devastation; mountains; the ocean; the numinous music of words; the endless festival of the senses; the excitement and beauty of woman; the joy of music; memories of hard but satisfying days of work on the bog, in the meadows, building walls; conversations that still sing in the mind; the harp cello of the Irish language; the Eucharist, and the celebration of the body in love; being listened to when words were frail and suffering was sore; the return of the swallows to the shed; my uncle's companionship; my father's mystical sense; and my mother's love and trust in my being.

AFTERWORD

ON SATURDAY, JANUARY 12, 2008, JOHN O'DONO-
hue was laid to rest in his beloved Co. Clare. It was a day
of celebration of a life, of lament for the loss of a loved one
and of wild Atlantic weather. That evening I wrote the
following words.

The Journey
FOR JOHN O'DONOHUE

We were promised a hard frost
But overnight a milder wind

Blew in from Fanore
And so we drove down ice-free roads
Through Kinvara and Bellharbour
A golden Burren sunrise
Heralded what you called
The wonder of the arriving day.

In Ballyvaughan a huge red sign
Pointed our way with just one word
FUNERAL

Around Black Head
The Atlantic's mighty sweep
Welcomed the growing line of cars
All with a single destination.

We parked amid the caravans
And walked along the singing river
Remembering how you envied it
Carried by the surprise
of its own unfolding

We gathered in the marquee
And delighted in greeting friends
With laughter and embrace
As you would wish

And no—none of us could take in
The reason we were here.

The obsequies began
Eucharistic mystery
Music and memory
And laughter, always laughter.

Des Forde invited us
To pay our respects
There would be no hurry
We would lay you to rest
When we were ready
And so we filed past your coffin
And laid hands on it.
And no—we couldn't take it in
We held your loved ones' hands
Wishing we could especially mind Josie
Proud and frail and broken.

And then the final, final stage
To Creggagh
A great caravan
Snaking along that wild
And surf-tossed shore
That thrilled you so

A vicious south-easterly
Whipped us with icy rain
And stung us to tears
As we lowered you to lie
Face to face with rock
In a limestone valley
Your soul already freed
Face to face with God
On the eternal mountain.

Charlie Piggott played
Éamonn an Chnoic
As we huddled
Báite fuar fliuch
For the last farewell.
Home now
Through the dying day
Down flooding roads
Past sodden fields
With one more stop to make
At Corcomroe
To remember Easter dawns
When you blessed the elements
And sang the risen Christ.

A silence
And then past

Weeping Burren flags
And through the shroud of mist
Descending
Into the dark.

John Quinn

Envoi

Sometimes
A voice is sent
To calm our deepest fears

Sometimes
A hearty laugh
Will banish all our tears

Sometimes
Words will wing
Our dreaming ever higher

And sometimes
A mind will set
Our imagining afire

John Quinn

IN MEMORIAM

THE STORY IS SILENT UNTIL THE WORD IS SPO-
ken and witnessed, and becomes flesh so that it can be
touched, felt and lived. The word germinates in the seduc-
tiveness of the dark until conversation tempts it towards
the dawn where the sun illuminates and gives witness and
seeing. Then, we, the human participants in the ongoing act of creation, can enable it to become flesh and live
amongst us. As this journey escalates, the arms of the out-
stretching Word embrace the entire world.

John O'Donohue's life cannot be encompassed within
the one act of birth, life and death. He was not a finite act
that existed and is now lost for evermore. He is a story that

is written and spoken and lives amongst us. Just as we are and continue to be.

His themes of echo as the response of continuity, imagination as the ability to still see the mountain behind the mist, and absence as the transformed presence of the vanished awaken our thinking and provide food for our spiritual journey in an increasingly hungry world.

One of the questions that John loved to pose was: "When was your last great conversation with someone?" Good conversation is the enemy of falsity, facade and shallowness. It chases the truth of things, it demolishes the flimsy foundation of facade and it penetrates the depths so as to soar into unfolding possibility. When things stay separate and isolated they stiffen into the act of surviving, whereas when they have a conversation with each other they begin to live as the artists of their own destiny.

The moment that two questioning minds and hearts meet in really great conversation, a portal opens into immensely exciting possibility.

So it is with this beautiful presentation by John Quinn: he tempts the reader to join him in a really great conversation with John O'Donohue. He introduces the conversation with a wonderful memory and weaves together some of John's favorite themes into a beautiful flow of mystical unfolding. The two Johns shared a wonderful thirst to sup from the chalice of imagination, which allows a different lens with which we can view all that is given. Whether in a bar, a radio station or an office or up a mountain, all these places were made sacred because of their meeting; "For where two or three meet in my name, I shall be there with them" (Matthew 18:20).

There is a wonderful freshness of spontaneity and chance about these encounters, yet John Quinn skillfully interlaces these conversations into a beautiful pattern.

On a personal note I must say that when not up a mountain, if you could sit my brother in a dimly lit pub with a pint and a cigar and inadvertently present the well-sculpted question, then you would be carried into the surprise of the unfolding, unstemmable flow.

John used to always advise me to write down or record all the wonderful statements made by my children when they were discovering language as a means of expression. He would explain how they had come from the other world into our dimension and how their memory of that world had not yet faded, so the color of their statements was an echo of memory of the place from which they were given to us!

Because I am here,
Where is it that I am absent from?

—John O'Donohue

Not alone should I have recorded them, I should also have recorded him!

As I look at my desk I see that I have the dictionary, the Bible and *Benedictus* open for help, yet my eye is drawn out the window to the landscape, which was such a profound inspiration for John. It led him to the wonderful recognition of the "inner landscape," and so the magic began.

This wonderful book by John Quinn contains a lot of unpublished material and two beautiful poems by his own hand, which celebrate my brother and mourn his passing. The section on "Dawn Mass" was an impromptu recording and just happened by chance—if there is such a thing! I think that if you can be present to the wonder of the heart, it always knows the secret and can lead us to the "where" and "when," and then we introduce the "why" and call it "chance." Thanks to John Quinn just being there, we have become witnesses to something magical.

The Eucharist was so special for John O'Donohue, and he had such a tremendous reverence and attraction towards Corcomroe Abbey in Clare. Here he led the most amazing "conversation in God" involving humans, nature and the dawn, in the presence of "the spirits of those who lived and prayed here for centuries." It is a Eucharist of almost tangible healing and light. Then towards the end of his homily is that sentence that put everything in perspective:

*We were sent here to search for the light of Easter in
our hearts, and when we find it we are meant to give
it away generously.*

As you travel this Burren valley of John's birth, the
road meanders parallel to the river, guiding you out into
the world as the river carries its blessing to the sea. Of
course, just as the river enables the salmon to swim back
up at their time, so too does the road take you back up
away from it all, or as John used to say, "You can get in
out of it."

Either way, as you travel this path and you look up
at the sides of the valley as they climb to the horizon, all
you can see is barren limestone speckled with green. The
mind wonders how life could be sustained here, but if you
could be guided by the wonder of the heart and you took a
chance to cross the wall (without knocking it!) and climb,
you could be starting a pilgrimage. Hidden in the fissured
face of the mountain are surprising shelves of green show-
ing to the sky, which sustain and nourish the animals over
the bleak winter. Here you can gaze and graze in these
wondrous pastures and the conversation begins. In this
awakening you realize that, having tasted the mountains,
nibbling at the sides of the path will satisfy you no longer.

May we learn to return
And rest in the beauty

Of animal being,
Learn to lean low,
Leave our locked minds,
And with freed senses
Feel the earth
Breathing with us.

From "To Learn from Animal Being,"
To Bless the Space Between Us

Pat O'Donohue
(John's brother)

Tel: 091-57638

Seann Creasna,
Camus.

July 24. 2001.

Dearest John,

I have you in my mind so often in these last weeks. Thinking of the blade of loss that still cuts deeply into you. I feel such sadness for you. I was really sorry not to be able to join ye at the funeral. I had no choice as I had to be in Kerry. Lelia told me all. I believe you spoke wonderfully about the ripening complexity of Olive's soul & Seann spoke too. She would have loved that!! No one knows but you what you have lost & where in your heart it is lost from. Some of you has gone too. All that torn tissue outside the body in that "Betweenness" where ye met, were new stolen. It takes a lot of time to allow that to heal & return into you until the skin can become seamless again.

Grief is so awful – unpredictable, awkward & so so lonely. John – I am thinking about you. I am here & if there is any way I can help, I would be delighted. May all the kindness & care that you bring to the world & the Word return to shelter & heal you. & may you begin to sense how near you Olive is & that she is watching out for ye all in a secret & eternal way.

in Love, & in Cathy & friendship,

John O'Donohue

A letter from John O'Donohue to John Quinn on the passing of Quinn's wife, Olive.

ACKNOWLEDGMENTS

Blessings and extracts from *To Bless the Space Between Us* by John O'Donohue, published by Bantam Press, in 2007. Reprinted by permission of The Random House Group Limited. "Connemara in Our Mind," "Gleninagh," "November Questions" and "Cottage" by John O'Donohue are all taken from *Echoes of Memory*, published by Transworld Ireland. Reprinted by permission of The Random House Group Limited. "The Angel of the Bog" and "Thought-Work" by John O'Donohue are both taken from *Conamara Blues*, published by Bantam Press, in 2001. Reprinted by permission of The Random House Group Limited. John's talk at the 1999 Céifin Conference originally appeared in *Working Towards Balance: Our*

Society in the New Millennium (Céifin Conference Papers, 1999), published by Veritas in 2000. With thanks to the Céifin Conference. John's interview with Suzanne Power, published in the *Sunday Tribune* in 2005, appears by kind permission of the author.

Lines from "Advent" and "Father Mat" by Patrick Kavanagh are reprinted from *Collected Poems,* edited by Antoinette Quinn (Allen Lane, 2004), by kind permission of the Trustees of the Estate of the late Katherine B. Kavanagh, through the Jonathan Williams Literary Agency. "I Go Among Trees and Sit Still" by Wendell Berry, from *A Timbered Choir: The Sabbath Poems 1979–1997.* Copyright © 1998 by Wendell Berry. Reprinted by permission of Counterpoint. "The Art of Disappearing" from *Words Under the Words: Selected Poems* by Naomi Shihab Nye, copyright © 1995. Used with the permission of Far Corner Books, Portland, Oregon. Lines from *Crossing Unmarked Snow* by William Stafford, published by University of Michigan Press in 1998. Line from "Love After Love" by Derek Walcott, from *Sea Grapes: Collected Poems 1948–1984,* published by Farrar, Straus and Giroux in 1984. "Section: XIV" by Octavio Paz, translated by Eliot Weinberger, from *Eagle or Sun?,* copyright © 1969, 1970, 1975, 1976 by Octavio Paz and Eliot Weinberger. Reprinted by permission of New Directions Publishing Corp.

An extract from "The Journey—for John O'Donohue" by John Quinn originally appeared in his *Moments* (Veritas, 2011), and appears here in its entirety; "Envoi" by John Quinn appears here in print for the first time.

Every effort has been made to contact the copyright holders of the material produced in *Walking in Wonder: Eternal Wisdom for a Modern World*. If any infringement has occurred, the owners of such copyright are requested to contact the publishers.

ABOUT THE AUTHORS

John O'Donohue was a poet, philosopher and scholar, a native Gaelic speaker from County Clare, Ireland. He was awarded a PhD in philosophical theology from the University of Tübingen, with post-doctoral study of Meister Eckhart. John's numerous international best-selling books—*Anam Cara*, *Beauty*, *Eternal Echoes* and the beloved *To Bless the Space Between Us*, among many others—guide readers through the landscape of the Irish imagination.

John Quinn is a former broadcaster with RTÉ Radio (Irish National Radio). An award-winning writer of children's fiction, he has also authored/edited several other books, including an adult novel, two memoirs, and a number of books based on his radio work, notably *Walking in Wonder*. He lives in County Galway, Ireland.